# *The* Significance
## PRINCIPLE

# The Significance PRINCIPLE

## The Secret Behind High Performance People and Organizations

### DR. LES CARTER AND JIM UNDERWOOD

BROADMAN
&HOLMAN
PUBLISHERS
NASHVILLE, TENNESSEE

© 1998

by Les Carter and Jim Underwood

All rights reserved

Printed in the United States of America

0-8054-1664-1

Published by Broadman & Holman Publishers, Nashville, Tennessee

Page Design: Anderson Thomas Design

Editorial Team: Vicki Crumpton, Janis Whipple, Kim Overcash

Page Composition: TF Designs

Dewey Decimal Classification: 650.1

Subject Heading: COMMUNICATION IN ORGANIZATIONS/INTERPERSONAL COMMUNICATION

Library of Congress Card Catalog Number: 98-22599


**Library of Congress Cataloging-in-Publication Data**

Carter, Les.

The significance principle : the secret behind high performance people and organizations / Les Carter, Jim Underwood.

p. cm.

ISBN 0-8054-1664-1 (pb)

1. Communication in organizations. 2. Interpersonal communication.

I. Underwood, Jim, 1941–. II. Title.

HD30.3.C357 1998

650.1'3—dc21

98-22599

CIP


1 2 3 4 5 02 01 00 99 98

*To our wives, Jennifer and Patsy, our partners in life whose consistent encouragement is valued above all else.*

*To Dr. Fred Dow of U.S. International University, whose encouragement has touched lives around the world.*

*To those who have encouraged us along the road of life. You made a difference in our lives.*

# CONTENTS

# ACKNOWLEDGMENTS

We would like to thank all of the people who so willingly contributed their time and patience in helping us put this manuscript together. Perhaps most touching was the contribution of "Mom's family," Barbara Medlin and her sisters.

We discussed our ideas with such people as Zig Ziglar, Dan and Martha Weir, and Steve Grissom and they each enthusiastically contributed to our final work. Carolyne West's story touched our hearts and we wanted to recognize her leadership in the lives of those that many would have given up on.

Who could imagine the pressure that Tania Askins endured in having to translate all of our notes and comments as we wrote the book. Thank you for your contributions, Tania, and your work on the manuscript.

Our work with the staff at Broadman and Holman Publishers has been a real delight. This would not have been possible without Ken Stephens, Kim Overcash, Vicki Crumpton, and Janis Whipple. You guys are the best!

# INTRODUCTION

Over the past few years, we have had numerous opportunities to work with major organizations that were looking for ways to deal with sagging performance. Often, the key management team admitted to problems with "leadership" or "culture" and yet, when it came to understanding how to deal with these issues, they generally had no clue how to solve these problems.

After conducting over fifty graduate school studies of major firms, most of them Fortune 500 companies, we have consistently found that almost all had major deficiencies in the leadership area. In many cases, those same firms' annual reports tout the company's attitude of "empowerment" toward their employees. Yet, when we had the opportunity to talk with some of those employees, empowerment was the last word they thought of in trying to describe how they were treated.

In one story told to us by the internal consultants for a major international firm, they recounted how they had identified senior leadership's style as one of the key problems affecting the firm's competitive abilities. In their presentation to the senior executives, everything went well until they got to the problem of executive leadership. To quote one of the internal consultants: "Their conclusion was that they were righteous. They decided that the real problem was the middle managers. They totally rejected the possibility that they were the problem."

There are two ironies in this situation: First, in spite of years of research and the writing of books about management and leadership, little has been written about how to effectively lead people. Management books and organizational behavior books develop research into theories about management. But they do little to address the "how" of leadership.

The other irony is just as pervasive in nature. While a lot of managers talk about accountability, rarely if ever, do they talk about making managers accountable for their behaviors. A popular saying today is "managing to the quarter." The idea is that senior managers manage their operations so that they maximize the firm's quarterly profits for Wall Street. The problem is, such management approaches tend to destroy the long-term profit output of the firm. How? It's simple. In reality, it is the people of an organization which produce the profit. "Managing for the quarter" tends to sacrifice a firm's people in the interest of a short term goal. In the long term, competent, capable performers are unwilling to put up with such behavior. They usually leave the firm, and after a while the firm is left with an entire team of what might be called the "bottom 50 percent of the talent pool" comprising 100 percent of the firm's workforce.

What we have discovered about organizational performance is simple: Long term profit and performance is driven by how you treat people. Yet, organizations generally fail to make managers, as well as non-managers, accountable for the behavior which produces organizational performance. All of the teaching of management theories cannot change how someone treats someone else. We found that most assessments of individuals rarely measure the performance-producing behaviors critical to driving success and organizational renewal.

As a result of our investigation, we felt that we needed to develop our own assessment instruments, which clearly focused on the key performance factors. Once developed, we then began to go into organizations and assess both management and non-management personnel. It should be no surprise that the high performing people scored high on our assessments and the low performing people scored low. In principle, the high performing people excelled in how they valued and treated others. The reverse was also true.

At one major firm, we had an opportunity to really see how important our discovery was. We assessed about thirty people, both managers and non-managers. In one case, a senior executive scored so well that we almost did not believe the results. In still another, a non-management contributor's assessment revealed that she had serious interpersonal skills problems. After our seminar was over, we asked for a confidential evaluation of the two people.

The senior executive who had scored so high deserved his ratings. He was known as a man who was humble, and absolutely rejoiced over the success of his people. The non-management contributor, who received the lower scores, was one who found it necessary to demean everyone below her.

We also found that there are some companies that insist on very high standards of leadership from their people. The time we spent at Southwest Airlines was a real encouragement. Of all of the companies we dealt with in writing the book, they really are committed to "walking the talk."

The book is written in three general sections. First, we talk about relationships and the basics of high-performance relationships. It is in this section that we lay the foundation for all applications of *The Significance Principle*.

The second section addresses techniques for changing personal behaviors. As the reader will note, change begins with the individual. Only then, can we expect others to change.

The third section deals with application. High performance teams, executives, managers, and sales are all addressed. This is not a book we wrote for just managers or just individual contributors. This is a book designed to address all levels of the organization.

One of the firms cited in this book was recognized as the top company to work for in the U.S. in 1998. If we were to describe in one idea what this book is all about, it is about how to create just such a company.

Another thing occurred as we asked different people from major companies to review the manuscript. One statement seemed to be made over and over after people read the book. That statement was: "I would love to work for a company where I was treated like this." We hope that after reading this book, you will commit to making your company just such an organization—a place where people love to work because of how you treat them.

P.S. If you make the commitment, you might discover some profit benefits as well.

## Chapter *One*
# CREATING WINNING RELATIONSHIPS

As the young woman turned to take her next customer's order, her manager walked over to her. "From now on," he shouted for everyone to hear, "put the napkins on the upper shelf so we can reach them! It's a lot easier to reach them there." Then he turned and walked away, sneering. An observer couldn't help but wonder, *Is this what they teach at Taco University?*

The young woman was embarrassed and a coldness crept into her eyes . . . the look that might be seen in the eyes of abused children, the look of being disconnected. This woman, feeling unnecessary shame and hurt, became a participant in a losing relationship. And the manager was helping to create a low-performance organization.

What was happening here? The young lady, probably looking for a break in an entry-level job, was being denied a status of significance. The manager, apparently seeking to stroke his own status needs, chose to dismiss the employee's dignity and elevate himself at her expense. No doubt, he did this unconsciously; he did not set out to rob the employee of her significance. But intentional or not, the damage was done. He added a losing dimension to their relationship.

There is a real object lesson here. The manager at the taco restaurant and the employee he verbally abused probably started out their relationship with the highest of expectations. They might have talked about being part of a team and how she could work her way into management. But as time passed and the manager's pattern of forcing his preferences at the employee's expense emerged, the goal of team spirit evaporated.

How many times a day do you suppose this pattern of communication occurs? Whether the setting is a fast-food restaurant or the board room of a Fortune 500 company, we are often oblivious to the damage being done in our communications with fellow employees. For various reasons, one person fails to acknowledge the significance of another. Maybe stress is a major culprit. Perhaps the communicator is an insecure control freak building self's ego at the other person's expense. It could be that the communicator has been sitting on top of anger created by a history of pain and disappointment.

Whatever the reason, lost in the strains and tensions of life is the person's need to feel as if she matters, that she is somebody, that she fits in. Most communicators of nonsignificance do not *intend* to detract from others' significance; they simply do not recognize what's taking place. Yet the problem can be turned around, if a person so chooses. With some personal restructuring, losing patterns of relating can give way to winning patterns. It can start with you!

## What a Word of Encouragement Can Do

Over forty years ago a young salesman was struggling just to get by. After two and a half years with his company, he had learned all the skills of how to get prospects, make appointments, conduct demonstrations, handle objections, and close the sale. Yet he was not getting the job done. At one point his home phone was disconnected and the electricity cut off. When his wife gave birth to their first child, he had to scramble to make two sales to get the baby released from the hospital.

At a sales meeting in Charlotte, North Carolina, this young man encountered an older gentleman who had been watching him and who believed he had great potential. He pulled the salesman aside for a private conversation and told him he had the ability to be national sales champion and someday he should be an executive in the company . . . if he just believed in himself and worked from an organized schedule. These were foreign words to the salesman, yet his respect for his mentor caused him to take them to heart and actually live as if they might be true.

Prior to this conversation, the salesman had seen himself as "a little guy from a little town." The tenth of twelve children, he had been raised by a single mother whose husband died early. An average high school student with only a few minor accomplishments, he had tried his hand at college but quickly dropped out, hoping to make it big in the world of business. At the time his mentor spoke with him, this young salesman was riddled with personal doubts.

Yet that conversation began a remarkable turnaround. After the talk, he developed an entirely different picture of himself. This talk "gave me a tremendous boost in confidence and self-acceptance, and for the first time in my life, hope was born," he said. "My hopes were high so I worked harder and asked prospects to buy more often. In overcoming my doubts about my future, I was able to overcome the inhibitions and reluctance to work hard and make the effort to get the sale."

By the end of that year, the salesman had risen from obscurity to become number two of the seven thousand salespersons in the company. He received a promotion to management, then the next year became the company's highest paid field manager in the country. Two years later he became the youngest divisional supervisor in the company's sixty-six-year history. He determined never again to be a "little guy from a little town" struggling for survival, but instead would strive to accomplish much.

This salesman, Zig Ziglar, is recognized today as a leading authority in motivation and personal training. An author of several books, he has spoken internationally before audiences of thousands. Chances are, you've heard of Zig, the little guy from Yazoo City, Mississippi, who made it big.

But do you know P. C. Merrell?

P. C. Merrell was the man who saw something in Zig that Zig did not see in himself. It was P. C. Merrell who took it upon himself to guide a young man who needed an encouraging word. Seeing beyond the numbers game that accompanies quotas and monthly reports, P. C. Merrell saw the person, a young man with talent who had not yet learned to tap into his own significance, his value to both customers and the company.

Have you ever known a P. C. Merrell? Has someone ever said to you, "I believe in you"?

Or have you ever been someone's P. C. Merrell? Are you the type of person who actively seeks out people in order to touch them at the inner place of value?

At the core of organizational performance is relationships, whether between peers or between managers and subordinates. When these relationships feature consistent, encouraging messages, plans succeed. But when these relationships do not build significance, disaster can result. Consider the following:

- In research developed by Scott Degraffenreid, a forensic accountant, a high correlation between the *negative nature* of management-subordinate relationships and organizational failure was observed. (Similar relationships were developed related to *employee turnover*.)

- In research completed for a Fortune 100 firm by Dr. John Bassler, implementation of a relationship-profiling subordinate review of managers resulted in significant improvement of the following factors: *employee satisfaction; customer satisfaction;* and *unit performance.*

- The July 29, 1997, edition of the *Dallas Morning News* cited research from England that correlated high-stress management-subordinate relationships and the incidence of heart attacks.

- In hundreds of studies conducted by Dr. H. Igor Ansoff and his associates, statistically validated relationships have been developed between positive, empowering organizational management and higher return-on-investment.

## The Drive for Significance

It is our belief that each person lives with an inborn desire to be significant. In fact, every aspect of human behavior, both positive or negative, can be directly traced to the pursuit of personal significance. Depression, anger, and impatience are just some of the ways that people illustrate their yearning for significance. Likewise, loyalty, reliability, and responsibility are driven by the hope that significance can be sustained.

For example, the individual who works hard to get through college with a high degree of integrity intact should be congratulated.

He sought to be significant and was successful. At the same time, the person who behaves contrary to the needs of the family, organizations, friends, and the community may have a problem that can be understood in the light of his need to find a place of significance. His problems cannot be adequately resolved until the matter of significance is fully addressed.

Consider the famous marathon runner who left the race course, ran off a bridge, and fell into a ravine. Spectators could not believe she would intentionally do such a thing. It turned out that when she realized she was going to lose the race, she decided the only way she could avoid feeling like a complete loser was to "have an accident." Her need for significance was so strong that it drove her to seek an inappropriate solution. She survived the fall and later got the help she needed to resolve her feelings.

Can you relate to such a need? Have you ever felt compelled to cover up wrongs? To impress others with your achievements? To do whatever it took to make the grade? Of course you have. Much that drives you, much that drives the people you know, is anchored in the desire to be held in the best light possible.

### The Significance Principle

*The basic, driving force of human behavior is the desire for acceptance, understanding, appreciation, and recognition. The need for significance is such a powerful aspect of our personality that it motivates us to identify with success and just as powerfully motivates us to avoid failure and conflict.*

As soon as you entered the world, you screamed and cried. In essence, you said: "Hey, somebody needs to take care of me now." When someone wrapped you in a warm blanket and held you securely, you calmed down and added, "Now there, that's more like it." In the days to follow you repeated many such messages hundreds, even thousands of times.

What prompted you during your first moments of life to communicate so powerfully? The significance principle. Instinctively you felt a need, a right, to be held in high regard. You were searching for someone to tell you: "I think you're important," or "You have value," or "Your needs are legitimate." You wanted to feel significant and you responded to the actions of those around you who recognized your need.

What would you think about a person who, at the moment of your birth, set you aside with no hugs, no tenderness, no caretaking, and then said, "As soon as you accomplish something, I'll treat you with significance . . . but not one moment sooner." You'd cry foul! That's no way to treat an infant. In fact, such calloused behavior would be labeled abusive, even criminal.

Inherent in every life is a God-given value and worth. At the moment life begins, our Creator gifts individuals with significance. Instinctively you know you deserve it, and at some level of awareness you know others do too.

Consider carefully how the significance principle is at the foundation of many qualities, both good and bad. Can you detect how it is at the core of each of the following examples?

- In a routine social conversation, a friend exaggerates his accomplishments, hoping for a few extra pats on the back.

- A student pushes herself to maintain an A average, driven by the need to prove herself as acceptable and respected.

- A rookie employee feels she must be mistake-free in order to prove her worth to peers.

- A tyrannical manager feels he has to be perceived as a notch above his subordinates.

- A salesperson is calculating in what she says to her field supervisor, knowing that the wrong words could bring accusations of company disloyalty.

- A marketing executive feels he has to lower personal moral standards in order to keep the business of the customer he is entertaining.

- A worker cuts corners, knowing his boss will be angry if a project is not completed on time.

- In routine conversations with friends, a person talks freely about personal successes, yet rarely reveals personal flaws or struggles.

Can you see in each example how people can be pushed to behave as they do, based on the possibility of being either denied or given significance? This factor silently underlies many of the choices we make every day. Only as we become aware of the centrality of the significance principle can we begin to understand why we do what we do.

Are you aware of how your own decisions are influenced by your need to feel significant? Do you realize how powerfully your relations with others would be affected if you could consistently help them feel significant?

By gaining an awareness of the significance principle, we have the opportunity to turn losing relationships into winning relationships.

Return now to the manager of the taco restaurant. We'll not fault him for seeking cleanliness and order. But armed with an awareness of the significance principle, he could have pulled the employee aside and calmly said, "I like the way you're catching on to our procedures. There are so many small details to learn, who would have thought of all of them before actually working here! Help the rest of the crew by putting the napkins on the shelf we can all reach. You've got a great spirit and I appreciate your willingness to learn!"

How hard would that be? In fact, you may now be thinking, *Seems like a piece of cake. Anyone can do this significance thing.* With that in mind . . .

Who in your world would benefit if you led the way in living out the significance principle? Your customers? The clerical staff? Subordinates at work? Your boss? Family members? The guy in the car in front of you? The check-out clerk at the supermarket?

*Knowing* the significance principle is simple enough. *Living* with it as a guide, being aware of its many applications, is another story. To consistently apply it, you will need to honestly assess your behaviors and attitudes.

To help you gain a broader understanding of the ways the significance principle can affect your lifestyle, we have compiled a list of ten qualities valued by most true builders of significance. To how many can you relate?

## THE TEN VALUES OF SIGNIFICANCE BUILDERS

1. **They practice humility.** *They enter relationships with a realistic understanding of their own shortcomings and a realization that they, too, are human.*

2. **They proactively focus on others.** *They seek to understand the needs and perspectives of others.*

3. **They practice integrity.** *They understand that honesty and trustworthiness are bedrock qualities of any successful relationship.*

4. **They deal positively with conflict.** *They realize that moments of conflict, when handled in a positive manner, can be turned into opportunities for improved communication.*

5. **They live the significance paradox.** *They understand that true success is the result of first affirming the significance of others.* *They put team goals ahead of personal goals.*

6. **They openly encourage others.** *They understand the life-changing power of encouragement.*

7. **They use ceremony to recognize others' significance.** *They understand that the public recognition of others' accomplishments and qualities is one of the most important ways of affirming their significance.*

8. **They commit to personal accountability.** *They develop relationships with those who will help them maintain pure motives and right relationship skills.*

9. **They actively work to right wrongs.** *They willingly accept feedback and look for ways to repair damage that might have been caused by their own actions.*

10. **They are committed to excellence.** *They realize the quality of their work often serves as the starting point for others' success.*

## "Waitress!"

A number of years ago a waitress named Nancy worked in a Dallas seafood restaurant. Nancy was friendly, resourceful, and most of all, customer-focused. When customers had a special request, Nancy went out of her way to get the job done and help her customers feel satisfied.

If you were privileged to sit in Nancy's area of the restaurant, you would quickly learn that there really weren't any "rules" about ordering from the menu. If you wanted shrimp and steak, even though it wasn't on the menu, she would take your order and then "negotiate" with the chef. In a few minutes your steak and shrimp would arrive, exactly as you asked for it.

At lunch time when the business community hit restaurant row, two waiting lines instead of one snaked into the restaurant . . . one for Nancy's area and the other for the rest of the restaurant. Nancy's line was almost always longer than all of the other waiters' combined. Can you understand why?

Nancy took what most people would view as a tough and "less than significant" job and made it something special. She was committed to a higher standard and had to work harder than her peers to achieve the excellence she achieved. Nancy did not get her significance from her title, nor did she get it from her office or her clothes. She affirmed her significance by making her job a joy and an accomplishment and also realized that her customers had every right to be treated with significance.

Nancy retired a few years ago. Her professionalism enabled her to make a nice living and she was able to retire comfortably. Her customers, who had also become her friends, hated to see her go. She was the best!

Nancy had learned that she was valuable because she had something to offer—her kindness and her "can-do" spirit. Because she believed in herself, she was pleased and compelled to elevate her customers to VIP status. No one in her world deserved anything less than the best she could offer.

## How the Significance Principle Affects Our Personal Development

Unfortunately, the story does not always play out so nicely in other places of business. Have you ever associated with someone who seemed to go out of the way to communicate in hurtful ways? In many instances there is nothing wrong with the maligned person or service; the accuser is simply intent on creating problems. The critic's felt lack of significance blinds him from seeing others' need for significance.

Difficult people often search for significance in a perverse way. They demean someone they consider "safe". . . a person who can't easily fight back . . . in order to give themselves a temporary "significance fix." But notice something interesting: While the critic may often appear to be assertive and confident, in reality he or she is expressing a high level of fear that others will deem him or her insignificant.

When someone attempts to find significance by discounting others, he does not attain significance at all but a shallow smugness that soon fades. To keep alive the illusion of importance, the person must continue to undercut others.

If you want the significance principle to work consistently for you, beware of seeking significance where it cannot be found. For instance, do you struggle with any of the following?

- Being bossy
- Holding onto racial or gender prejudices
- Getting even when you feel you've been wronged
- Refusing to talk, especially when someone wants to hear from you
- Spreading gossip behind someone's back
- Interrupting another's speech to inject your "better" ideas
- Being critical
- Workaholism
- Perfectionism
- Airing your anger in a cutting tone of voice

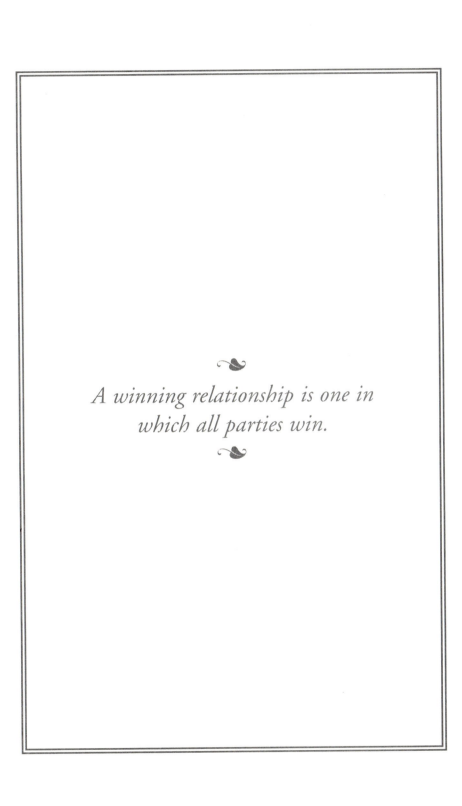

*A winning relationship is one in
which all parties win.*

- Procrastinating because you've got better things to do
- Being sexually seductive or manipulative
- Stubbornly insisting on how right you are
- Sarcasm

We can attempt to find our own significance while ignoring that of others . . . but such efforts will inevitably fail.

Consider instead how to communicate significance in a real and lasting sense. By becoming aware of significance-based communication and by committing yourself to the "ten values of significance builders," you can expect to successfully live out the significance principle. How many of the following qualities usually characterize you?

- A calm, confident demeanor
- Recognizing when others are stressed and responding helpfully
- Being patient
- Paying sincere compliments
- Openly sharing gladness over someone else's success
- Remembering simple preferences of others
- Taking time to slow down and talk about personal matters
- Using an even tone of voice during a confrontation
- Enjoying a reputation as steady and reliable
- Regularly commenting on what is right and good
- Being willing to solicit input during decision-making times
- Expressing tenderness naturally, saying the words "I love you" or "I appreciate you" sincerely
- Admitting when you're wrong, without excessive shame

- Being a genuine encourager, a positive presence
- Knowing when to speak and when to be silent
- Committing to the ethical treatment of others

These few examples demonstrate that significance can be expressed in an endless variety of ways. Are you ready to become committed to significance as a way of life?

## The Power of Significance

A number of years ago a minister was interviewed on a national radio program about his belief that people can often be the most effective communicators of godly encouragement. He described a two-hour layover at the Seattle airport in which he began to recall his fourth grade teacher.

He remembered struggling in this teacher's class because he was unwilling to work as hard as she expected. On one occasion, she pulled him aside and expressed her concern that he was not trying very hard and that he was capable of much more. She also declared she was unwilling to let him get by with mediocre work. His next few weeks were miserable as she appeared to raise her expectations ever higher. Finally, in a fit of anger, he decided to show her by spending extra hours on an assignment. All he wanted was to get her off his case. But when she responded with praise and recognition, he liked it so much that he continued to do good work. This carried over to his other classes. That lone teacher encouraged him to become a good student and he began to excel academically.

As he sat in the airline terminal, the thought struck him that she had once expressed her belief in his God-given abilities. *Now,* he thought, *it's my turn.* He looked for her name in the phone book, found it, and called the listed number. A creaky voice answered and he soon discovered the woman who had been his teacher . . . and she even remembered him.

He spent several minutes describing what she had done for him. He declared that her efforts in getting him to use his potential had turned his life around and that he could trace much of his success as a minister and as a person to her interest in him. For the longest time there was no response . . . until he heard quiet sobbing at the other end of the line.

"I hope I have said nothing to hurt you," he quickly said.

"You haven't hurt my feelings," she gently replied. "I taught for forty-three years, but this is the first time anyone took the time to tell me that my efforts made a difference in their life. I appreciate it so much."

Most of us never take the time to recognize the significance of others, even when we have benefited enormously from their encouragement. The schoolteacher needed to hear that someone saw her as necessary, as someone who mattered. Though she did not need her former student's reinforcement to maintain her significance, it certainly helped. This woman's grateful reaction showed the minister the immense importance of communicating significance to others . . . and he became all the more committed to the fundamental truths of his spiritual life.

## It's Up to You

You can choose to follow the minister's example. You can choose to act in ways that highlight the value and dignity of others. Whether in a boardroom or a loading dock, people need to hear the valuable message, "I recognize your unique qualities and I hope to partner in your success by affirming your value by my actions."

Businesses spend millions (if not billions) of dollars to improve corporate performance. While they must give attention to changing trends and organizational efficiency and improved procedures, they will ultimately fail if they ignore the significance of their people! And it's not enough to give lip service to this critical practice; maximum performance cannot be achieved unless people's significance is openly acknowledged.

Consider a story told by Jaime Escalante, whose life is depicted in the movie *Stand and Deliver*. Escalante changed the educational paradigm in a California ghetto school district. He took children from backgrounds of poverty and taught them calculus so well that many of them earned college credit for their work. But there is more to the story. Escalante once told how he learned to get his kids to perform, to want to improve their lives. "The Two Johnnys" taught him the critical lesson.

One evening Escalante had stayed at school late for a PTA meeting when a woman approached him and asked, "How is my Johnny doing in your class?" This created a problem, because he had two Johnnys in his class, quite different from one another. One was carrying a solid F+ and the other a solid A+. One was a constant disruption while the other was a joy. He thought for a moment and concluded that this must be "good Johnny's" mother. "He's great," he replied. "He is such a joy to have in class, he's always early, never disruptive, and does really good work. You should be proud of him."

The next day, "bad Johnny" walked up to his desk. "Mr. Escalante," he said, "I appreciate what you told my mother about me. I promise I will do my best to make what you said about me come true." It didn't take long. He went from failing, to making Cs, and finally he made the dean's list.

What Escalante discovered by accident is the truth of the significance principle. As we affirm the significance of others, we encourage them to improve their performance. By recognizing their significance, we appeal to that which drives their very existence: the desire to be recognized, the desire to be appreciated, the desire to be important. In short, the desire to be significant.

"Okay, you've made your point," you may be saying. "Significance is something that drives all of us. But where do I go from here?"

In the next chapter we will challenge you to take a hard look at yourself as you explore how you find your own significance. But before we do, let's ask ourselves how and why we respond to others as we do. Consider the following questions as honestly as you can.

## SIGNIFICANCE BUILDING: A PERSONAL ASSESSMENT

- *When was the last time you complimented a competitor in front of someone else?*

- *When was the last time you made a mistake, only to have someone focus on that mistake to the exclusion of all your prior good deeds? How did that make you feel?*

- *Describe the last time you built someone else up at your own expense.*

- *How do you feel when someone is a true encourager to you?*

- *How do you feel when encouragement should come your way, but does not?*

- *How would your life change for the better if you maintained a greater awareness of your own significance needs?*

# Chapter Two
## THE SIGNIFICANCE PARADOX

One of the most difficult challenges facing business people is hostility. A friend recently told us about her nightmarish experience with a group of union employees in New York.

She had been asked to replace a sick instructor for a customer service training class and immediately faced the group's sarcasm. At one point, a participant offered her view of customer service: "The first thing you have to do is make sure the customer understands that you're the boss and you won't take any junk off of them. If you don't put them in their place early, they will get the idea that they are in control. You just can't let that happen." Our friend asked us, "How do you handle a room full of people like that?"

We explained that by applying the significance principle effectively, even hostile situations can be defused and made to work. Let's view a snapshot from the life of a college professor named Carolyne West and see how she did just that.

Most college students give their professors at least a measure of respect, since they are generally more mature than high schoolers and have freely chosen to further their education. Most, but not all. Carolyne West, a veteran teacher of twenty-seven years, sized up one of her health education classes at Hartnell College in Salinas, California, early one fall semester and quickly realized she was in for an instructor's nightmare.

Students routinely talked while she talked and few seemed remotely interested in showing respect for her or their classmates. Carolyne determined not to let them discourage her and decided to assess her students to uncover the source of the problem. She soon realized that out of about forty students, three were instigators of private conversations, with about two followers each. The three groups were composed of three tough-acting white female teens, three Hispanic "gang-type" males, and three male athletes of mixed ethnicities.

Beyond that, about fifteen students appeared to have little interest in the subject matter or in attending college. Carolyne concluded that these disengaged students had enrolled merely to satisfy their parents; college was simply a way to continue to live at home rent-free. The remaining students appeared to want to learn, but the disruptive class atmosphere made it extremely difficult to meet their needs.

Only two weeks into the semester, Carolyne felt as though she had lost control of her class. She tried numerous techniques to provide an efficient and interesting learning environment . . . including small group activities, asking students to report on readings, and repeatedly asking unruly students to be quiet . . . but nothing worked. The rude disruptions continued. Four frustrating weeks into the semester, Carolyne resolved to settle the matter even if it meant "disenrolling" eight or nine students.

About this time, Carolyne happened to speak with the three Hispanic young men as they left class. With nothing to lose, she tried to enlist their help. Approaching them with respect and concern, she first asked why they had elected to take her class. She also discussed some options she was considering to deal with the problem. She made it clear she wanted a more positive solution and asked them to think about what they thought should be done. What would they do if they were in her place? She let them know she cared about their opinions and wanted to understand them better, and she promised to ask about their solution after the next class.

The following week the three young men made a couple of suggestions, and although they weren't workable, Carolyne could tell they were thinking. She thanked them and told them she valued their input, then invited them to come by her office anytime to discuss further ideas or just to chat about life. The very next day, all three young men showed up at her office to "check it out." Soon, they each began coming individually to talk with her. They found a good listener in Carolyne, who showed them respect and a willingness to understand their struggles.

Shortly afterward, Carolyne noticed something in class had changed: it was actually quiet. Students listened intently to her and to classmates with a question or comment. The three young men had become class zealots. They began strongly encouraging the few remaining disruptive students to be quiet so they might hear and be able to concentrate. Some of Carolyne's worst-behaved students had been transformed into her best allies!

Carolyne credits her success to a simple fact: When we make other people important by showing them respect and understanding, they will be more likely to reciprocate. In Carolyne's words, "The use of the significance principle allowed me to create a 'win-win' for everyone involved." To date, two of these three young men have continued to pursue their college degrees. One retook her class the following semester to earn a better grade; he realized he had not applied himself during the first part of the course. The second time around, he displayed one of the best attitudes in class and completed the course with an A.

Carolyne witnessed what we call "the significance paradox," and she became convinced that every teacher could benefit from applying the principle to each student.

---

### The Significance Paradox

THE WAY TO FIND YOUR OWN SIGNIFICANCE IS TO ACTIVELY RECOGNIZE THE SIGNIFICANCE OF OTHERS.

---

Let's consider this key thought by examining the impact of P. C. Merrell in the life of Zig Ziglar. As Zig's successes became commonplace, he often revisited that moment when Mr. Merrell expressed belief in him. Rather than thinking, *I've made it, therefore I can sit back and relax,* the thought grew in Zig's mind that *Someone instilled a sense of significance in me, so now I'd like to look for opportunities to give it away to others.*

Zig explains it this way: "In my current position as a writer, speaker, and owner of a business, virtually everything I do is aimed at growing and encouraging people. I daily make every effort to give the people with whom I associate legitimate hope, and since encouragement is the fuel upon which hope runs, I constantly look for ways to encourage them so their own worth and significance will be enhanced. To this day when I speak, I always ask God to make me the P. C. Merrell in the lives of those to whom I speak."

Do you suppose Zig is emotionally depleted once he searches out people to encourage? Hardly! To the contrary, his own significance is further solidified as he seeks to give it away. That's the significance paradox.

## Be Willing to Affirm Others

Whatever your level of interaction with people, you will improve your success by recognizing that each person needs to feel wanted. But how many distractions work against this recognition! A thousand other thoughts constantly vie for your attention. Notice, instead, what gets our attention as we interact with others:

- The end results of a task to be completed

- How the task is going to be performed

- Who else will be involved in the task

- What we are going to receive, based on other persons' actions

- How our plans will be affected

- How other people will perceive us

- How much time will be involved in completing a task

- The disagreements we have regarding another person's style

- How the information we receive reminds us of a similar incident from times past

- Our opinions about how a performance should be handled

Do you get the idea? We can give our attention to virtually anything but the significance of the person in front of us. When these matters dominate personal interaction, they can reduce individuals to "doers" only, with little regard for the person inside. Lost in the push to achieve can be the realization that the person in our presence has a need to feel valued and respected, and to be touched at an inner place of worth.

We will find greater influence and camaraderie when we remember that we are addressing a person, not a machine. Rather than thinking, *What are you going to do next for me?* we can think, *What is it about you that I can know and address?*

Of course, we cannot forget completely about performance; performance does factor heavily into any business pursuit. Yet we do not have to overlook the human element. People want to be thought of as people. They respond best when we balance our comments between performance and human issues.

Let's look at a few illustrations to suggest what we mean:

- Instead of saying, "You did a good job organizing the data for me," you might add, "I realize you've had several projects going at one time, which means you had to put out a special effort to get the job done. Your conscientious nature really shows."

- In addition to saying, "We've got to schedule a meeting with Mr. Smithers today," you can declare, "You have a way of talking with Mr. Smithers and defusing his tense personality. I truly respect you for that."

- When you say, "I'm really struggling to get this project done," you could comment, "This makes me appreciate your expertise on such a complicated subject."

- When you suggest, "Why don't we eat at the Italian restaurant today?" you might also add, "You're frequently considerate of my preferences, so I wanted to make sure we go to a place you enjoy."

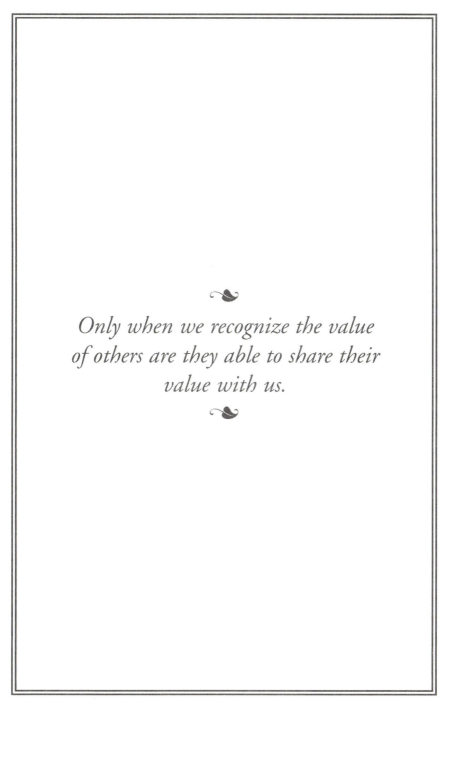

*Only when we recognize the value
of others are they able to share their
value with us.*

Each of these examples signifies a willingness to acknowledge the perspective of the other person, incorporating that perspective into your communication style.

Let's break the significance paradox down into four simple concepts:

1. Success is defined in terms of your ability to encourage others.
2. You receive significance messages from others in proportion to those you give to others.
3. You reject self-important practices and realize that character is more important than selfish gain.
4. You openly recognize your interdependence with others and recognize that the world does not revolve around you.

## What About Being Number One?

A plethora of books suggest that the only way to achieve real success is to make yourself *number one*. Others tell you to visualize yourself sitting in the CEO's chair or boarding the company jet to fly around the world to meet with heads of state. Have you ever known someone who would sacrifice anyone or do anything it took to be number one? How do you feel around people like that? You probably despise people who run over others to get ahead. Perhaps you've even been the victim of such behavior.

Is it okay to want to be number one? Is it okay to want to win? Is it okay to want to be the CEO of a firm and travel the world? Absolutely! The issue is *how* you plan to get there. Wanting to do your very best is a sign of character, since people of character are unwilling to "just get by." But here's the key: People of character are unwilling to win unless they take with them the people who helped get them to the top. People of character openly recognize their interdependence with others. That is why they are givers instead of takers.

Carolyne West learned that she enhanced her own significance when she built significance in others. As you follow her lead (or Zig Ziglar's, or P. C. Merrell's, or Nancy's), you will find that the only real success is founded in the four aspects of the significance paradox.

Do you remember the children's fable of King Midas, who wished that everything he touched would turn to gold? He received his wish, but found that in converting everything to gold, he lost the things most precious to him. That is what will happen to you, too, if you attempt to find your own significance while ignoring the significance of others.

Take a look at some of the ways we engage in significance-building as well as significance-destroying behavior. First, let's look at the ways we fail to recognize the significance of others. We call them "Fifteen ways to mess up company morale," but they could be called, "Fifteen stupid things we all do from time to time."

## FIFTEEN WAYS TO MESS UP COMPANY MORALE

1. Do nothing to establish a friendly rapport with others.
2. Focus on what is wrong with others.
3. Be preoccupied with your own responsibilities.
4. Never give an unrestricted compliment. Use words like "except for" and "but."
5. Compare people with one another (or yourself) in a negative manner.
6. When someone mentions a personal success, "one-up" them with something you've done better.
7. If someone disagrees with one of your ideas, be sure you make them understand how stupid their idea is.

8. Interrupt people before they complete a thought or an idea.
9. Never admit a mistake, regardless of how obvious it was.
10. Hold others to a set of impossibly high standards.
11. Allow others' bad moods to affect your attitude.
12. If you don't understand what someone is saying, make it clear that he or she is really off base.
13. Never change your opinion about anything; it's a sign of weakness.
14. Expect a payback if you do something nice for someone else.
15. Let your rules be more important than relationships.

How often have you seen others act in this manner? And how often do you unwittingly do some of these things?

If you are serious about personal change, here is an opportunity to gain a good idea about how you are doing in the significance area. Make a list of the fifteen items above and carry them with you for a day. Once an hour, go through the list and put a check mark by the things you did. You might find this an eye-opening exercise.

## Realistic Expectations and the Significance Paradox

Let's suppose you go to work determined to apply all that you've learned on a really difficult individual. By the end of the week, you feel like a doormat. You probably have concluded that either you have wasted a week of effort or you have made a complete fool out of yourself. Think about the following quote:

> I CAN'T DRIVE NOBODY'S TRUCK BUT MY OWN.
> **Anonymous**

The quote reveals one of the keys to becoming a significance builder in the lives of others. More often than not, you will encounter "takers" who will devour your attempts to affirm their significance and expect still more, while giving nothing in return. You must realize that if others are to change, they must *want* to change. You cannot drive anyone else's truck but your own. That is why you must be prepared for the takers. You must commit to be a person of character, regardless of their attitude or their mood or their response to you.

## A State of Mind, Not a Technique

The significance principle is not a scheme to get ahead, nor will committing to it change your life in less than a week. To make a difference, you must make a lifelong commitment to live out the significance principle. It is possible to live out the principles in this book and not know even half of the good you do or the lives you positively affect. Living for self alone (even while "applying" the significance principle) cannot ultimately fulfill anyone. You will never be affirmed in your own significance unless you first commit to affirming the significance of others. It really is a paradox, isn't it?

But a key question is, how? How can you become a giver and not just a taker? Let's consider fifteen things we can do to build company morale.

### FIFTEEN WAYS TO BUILD COMPANY MORALE

1. Be the first to smile when you meet someone.
2. Focus on what is good in others.
3. Have a positive preoccupation with what others want to accomplish.
4. Learn to regularly recognize others.

5. See each person as unique, not as someone to be compared against others.
6. When someone mentions a personal success, celebrate with them.
7. Encourage those who disagree with your ideas, and demonstrate your sincerity by taking action on their good ideas.
8. Learn to listen. Always listen *past* where they finished.
9. Never fail to admit a mistake if you committed it.
10. Demonstrate your standards by living them out before others.
11. Choose to express a good attitude regardless of those around you.
12. If you don't understand something, admit it and take advantage of the opportunity to learn.
13. Be willing to change your opinion, just as you would like others to do the same.
14. Never do anything nice merely to receive a payback.
15. Maintain your ethics and your character, without being a rigid rule keeper.

Have you ever known anyone who lived like this? If so, were you excited about their friendship and your association with them? Is it any wonder that these types of people have broad influence?

When people truly sense that you *believe* they are important, that your affirming behavior is not just for show, everyone gains. An infectious, positive attitude can spread throughout your organization. When a corporate mind-set is built upon the significance paradox, watch out! The sky is the limit from that point forward.

A number of studies have suggested that the people who get promoted are those who get along well with others. Those who train sales professionals often say, "People buy from people they like." The truth is, genuine success and accomplishment comes when we live out a commitment to build significance into the lives of others. Without that commitment, we become little more than egocentric takers.

## A Whole Company that "Walks the Talk"

"Welcome aboard, ladies and gentlemen. We're going to be on our way to either Houston or San Francisco in just a minute. Oh, I've just been informed that the pilot thinks she can find Houston, so we're going there. I'm your friendly flight service person Rottweiler, and I'd like to introduce Golden Boy in the front section, with Dal Dalmation and the Pit Bull with him in the aft section of the plane. We all went to the dog show in Dallas today, and to put it mildly, we went to the dogs. Oops . . . look who just got on the plane, our fearless leader, Herb. Well, fasten your lap straps everyone, because here we go to Houston, you guys. . . ."

You may never have heard that exact flight announcement, but if you ever fly Southwest Airlines, don't be surprised if you hear something similar. And if Herb Kelleher, Southwest's CEO, did get on board, you probably would hear something very much like that. The people at Southwest Airlines have a lot of fun! They also work really hard. And passenger surveys reveal that Southwest Airlines consistently performs like no other. What is the company's secret?

An analysis of its success formula reveals three critical factors:

1.  The company thrives on people who constantly affirm the significance of others.
2.  The company thrives on fun.

3. The company thrives on a commitment to excellence in everything it does.

Let's take a look at each of these areas to get a clear picture of Southwest's philosophy and the important relationships between significance, fun, and excellence.

## People Who Constantly Affirm the Significance of Others

People who want to go to work for Southwest immediately find that there are not enough jobs to go around. If you are fortunate enough to get an interview, you may find yourself in a group . . . they want to see how well applicants relate to others. One executive smiled when he described this procedure. "If they are unable to show a genuine interest in other people during the interview," he said, "we know right then that they don't fit the Southwest mold. We interviewed a group not too long ago and at the end of the interview everyone on the team recognized that one guy was head and shoulders above the rest. He had an ability to relate to others that convinced us he would be a winner for us. Oh, by the way, we got him . . . and he's already been promoted to a higher position."

We often heard that "self-important people don't last too long here." Several stories followed about people who came into the firm, only to quickly leave because they would not treat Southwest's people the way the company insisted they be treated. (Who says the only thing that matters is the bottom line?) Another individual told how she had worked for a church before coming to Southwest. "You know," she said, "I just wish that the people I used to work for had taken lessons from Southwest. They treat people like our faith taught us we should treat people."

Dave Ridley, Southwest's Vice President of Marketing and Sales, said he had developed his own mission statement for

Southwest. "People Matter Most," he declared. "That defines the foundation of everything we do."

"What about vendors?" we asked. "You haven't talked about the people who sell to you."

"They are just as important," he replied. "To us, 'people matter most' relates to our people, their families, our customers, and those who sell to us. We focus on those four areas."

## FUN!

"We play hard and we work hard" is a frequent comment from Southwest associates. Fun is one way Southwest maintains its corporate humility, and the instigator is apparently Herb himself.

When a class of newly hired pilots is about to graduate, a Southwest tradition kicks in. Somehow these new employees realize that if they are to enter the hallowed halls of fun (Southwest), they have to try to out-do the pranks pulled by the previous new-hire class. Recently an entire pilot graduating class dressed up in diapers and went *en mass* to meet Herb . . . unannounced, of course. Such hilarious pranks send a message: "We try not to take ourselves too seriously."

## COMMITMENT TO EXCELLENCE

"We set very high standards," a senior executive at Southwest told us. "And if people aren't committed to excellence in their job, they just don't fit Southwest." Another executive declared, "When it comes to working hard and the ability to get along extremely well with people, we are encouraged to be extremely decisive during the probationary period." He said it was important for both the employee and the company to be sure that the new hire could meet the standards Southwest sets for every member of its team. "We're going to make mistakes in hiring," he continued. "We simply don't want to compound that mistake by keeping that person around. It's best for both parties to recognize the situation and move on."

The concepts of hard work and people-focus are solidly ingrained at Southwest. "If someone is not cutting it, the employee's peers get involved to make sure that he or she understands what is expected," one person told us. And to no one's surprise, Southwest Airlines has profit sharing for its employees. What else would you expect?

## The Bottom Line of the Significance Paradox

While writing this book we mentioned our basic idea to a group of senior-level managers attending a seminar. "Our premise," we explained, "is that how you treat your people goes straight to the bottom line." A lively discussion ensued and most of the participants immediately wanted a copy of our book in the hands of their superiors. Who doesn't want to be treated with respect?

An associate recently completed a study for a major international firm in which he asked subordinates to rate their supervisors. Various scales focused upon how employees perceived they were treated by their supervisor. Before the study began, each supervisor was given a copy of the assessment and was told that his/her incentive pay would be based upon the rating he/she received from subordinates. Unsurprisingly, the supervisors began treating their subordinates more as equals and became much more interested in them as individuals. Immediately it became apparent that the assessment dramatically changed how the supervisors dealt with their subordinates. But there is more. Look at what also happened:

- **Employee satisfaction** *increased substantially during the evaluation period.*

- **Customer satisfaction** *increased substantially during the evaluation period.*

- **Unit performance** *increased substantially during the evaluation period.*

The significance paradox is not merely an interesting idea; when practiced, it yields remarkable results. Everyone wins when we affirm the significance of those around us. The company wins, the customer wins, the stockholder wins, the employees win—everyone wins.

So if this principle is so powerful, why do so few organizations make their people accountable for how they treat others? As you read the next chapter, be prepared to discover and contemplate the single most important quality in finding significance.

## THE SIGNIFICANCE PARADOX

- *Take the "Fifteen Ways to Mess Up Company Morale" test by looking at yesterday. How did you treat people?*

- *Make a list of the reasons why you don't practice the significance principle in certain settings. See if you can explain your reason by using the significance principle as a standard or measure.*

- *Look at the "Fifteen Ways to Build Company Morale" and put a check by the things you do well.*

- *Look at the previous list and see if you can get some idea of where your weaknesses are in building good relationships. What things could you do to positively impact your attitude in some of these areas?*

*Chapter* Three
# THE #1 INGREDIENT FOR SIGNIFICANCE

Near the end of 1996, Kingston Technology Corporation, a California-based computer memory products maker, made headlines across the country. Three months earlier Japan's Softbank Corporation had agreed to pay $1.5 billion dollars for a controlling interest in the company, making its founders, John Tu and David Sun, enormously wealthy. But as exciting as the buyout was, that is not what made headlines.

At that year's office Christmas party, Tu and Sun announced to their 523 employees that they would be receiving $100 million in bonuses. Forty million would be paid immediately, with the remaining sixty million set aside for future bonuses. The average bonus amounted to slightly more than $76,000, while some were slated to receive up to $300,000.

Employees were thrilled . . . but not surprised. One employee explained, "Several times a year David and John just make these spontaneous gestures. There's an envelope on your desk and you open it and say, 'Thank God I work for this company.' Then you put the envelope away and start working twice as hard."

Tu said he could use only so much money for himself and added, "We want to do a lot of things to return to the community, the people who have made this possible."

John Tu and David Sun certainly fit the profile of significance builders. Not only do they believe their employees have tremendous value, but they back their beliefs with their checkbook. These two men exhibit a core quality that we all should emulate: humility.

Contrast the atmosphere at Kingston Technology with the milieu created by a large corporation's senior manager, whom we will call Mr. Bratton. Upon his retirement, two parties were held. One was the official "Thanks for all you have done" reception given to him at the company; the other was a "good riddance" party held privately by former subordinates whose only regret was that he had not retired years sooner.

One employee talked to a coworker about the "good riddance" party. "Have you heard about the unofficial celebration party they had after old Bratton retired?" he said. "I couldn't believe it, there were so many people there. I had no idea so many folks would be glad to see him go. We even had people fly in to spend the night! This party was sure different from the reception given by the CEO . . . all that garbage about a 'respected leader' and 'loved by all.' Did you know anyone who thought he was anything other than a tyrant and a jerk?"

Which scenario do you suppose is most common in today's workplace? Which scenario most likely surrounds you?

## Humility: The Most Powerful Personal Strategy

Bratton and those like him fail to understand that it is possible to have both positive relationships with subordinates *and* attain personal significance. Bratton had created a work environment where everyone understood the rules: Make sure you feed the boss's ego if you want to keep your job and get promotions. He could falsely assume he was significant based on his employees' presumed loyalty toward him. Ultimately, he began to believe that all the compliments he forced from subordinates were actually heartfelt. How could anyone want to live such a life?

Bratton is only one true illustration of a person living with blinders on. We could just as easily focus on a physician who steps all over his or her nurse's fragile ego, a teacher who condescends toward a student, or a salesperson who forgets his purpose as a customer servant. The same scenario is repeated in many ways in an endless number of arenas.

Of course, all of us are capable of self-deception. Have you ever blamed others for your problems in order to protect your fragile feelings of significance? Or have you ever invalidated someone's suggestion because you didn't want to hear an unflattering truth about yourself? Of course you have; we all have. Admitting the problem is the first step toward solving it.

## Characteristics of a Humble Person

So how can you avoid a problem like this? The answer is *humility.*

What does humility look like? The best way to understand it is to look around. What best describes the people you would call humble? More than that, do you know any highly successful people who are humble? What best describes them?

Many people have flawed notions of humility. They think humble people are pleasant but weak. They assume that humility requires they allow others to run roughshod over them and prevents them from resisting strong-willed adversaries.

But humility is not "doormat-ism." It does not require anyone to be treated poorly, nor does it forbid assertiveness or a firm response.

Humility is an attitude of personal modesty, which recognizes that self's priorities and preferences should be held in check so that others' needs can also be addressed. It describes a type of spiritual maturity, acknowledging that self is not God. Rather than focusing on self's agenda only, humility causes people to consider their needs in the context of the greater world.

At Kingston Technology, Mr. Tu and Mr. Sun looked beyond their own good fortune and determined to lavish good on their people. This is far too uncommon in business settings, where personal goals often supersede team goals. The same could be said for many social circles. Many people seem to have a knack for keeping the focus on their own subjects of interest, or perhaps they just have a hard time tuning in to others' perspectives or feelings. Humble people, however, are outwardly focused, realizing their priorities and their needs are not so central that they cannot also accommodate the interests of others.

Humility is the most important quality for the person in search of significance. Humble persons have a broader awareness because they want to see beyond their own needs. The word *balance* describes them best since they are neither too selfish nor too deferring. When a task is assigned to them, they are able to grasp their role within the entire scheme of things. Unlike people who worry about jockeying for prime assignments or for special treatment, humble people do not take themselves too seriously. A sense of community, not ego, seems to drive these people.

Don't you feel more comfortable dealing with a person who keeps his ego in check? Isn't it true that the humble person is the one who exudes true self-confidence? Humble people have no interest in finding a "significance" that harms others. Truly

*The foundation for any effective life strategy must be humility. Without humility there can be no ability to value the contributions of others.*

significant people do not fret about making themselves look significant; they are too tuned into the world around them to do that. The following story plays up that difference.

A Texas rancher and an Arkansas farmer shared property lines on the Texas-Arkansas border. The farmer and the rancher often ran into each other in town on Saturdays at the feed store. On one occasion, the Texas rancher was talking about his ranch. Not one to be humble, he looked at his audience of a dozen people and decided they needed to know how important he really was. "My ranch is so large, that if I get into my pickup truck at sunrise and start driving, I'm still on my property at sunset," he boasted. To which the Arkansas farmer replied, "I used to have an old truck like that, too. I finally sold it and got a new one that would run."

Just like that Texas rancher, you may sometimes feel the need to make sure other people understand your significance. Be careful, though! That can be the surest way of making yourself look the opposite. To apply the significance principle, you must overcome the tendency to manipulate people into confirming your personal significance. Look over the following list and determine to what degree humility characterizes your behavior.

- I can compliment a person who is also my competitor.

- When making decisions, I can set my ego aside and be objective.

- I have determined that my mission in life involves service to others.

- I can say "I'm sorry" or "I was wrong" with no excessive sense of shame or struggle.

- I think of myself as a servant, concerned about helping others to win.

- I associate with people from all sorts of socioeconomic or age groups.

- I am aware that my successes are almost always the result of a team effort.

- I am patient when others show imperfection, knowing that I, too, need others to be patient with me.

- When I make a point, I am typically firm while also considerate.

- If someone has something unflattering to say about me, I will hear it fully and consider it carefully.

- One of my greatest joys is in helping others succeed.

- I try to think of the big picture as I make my daily plans.

- Even as I maintain high standards and expectations, I accept others as they are.

- Behind my back, people say I'm approachable and fair-minded.

The qualities of a humble person are not the most natural or easy to sustain. In fact, when faced with everyday circumstances, humility seems almost impossible! Yet with determination and commitment, this trait can become central to your relational style.

## False Pride

By this point, you might think that the significance principle calls for a healthy dose of personal pride. Yet how can you have that pride while also being humble? It's a good question.

First, the issue is not pride, but *false* pride. When someone engages in nonedifying communication, when they belittle another's accomplishments, they exhibit false pride. And what exactly is "false pride"?

Drift back in time and remember when you were a child watching an old western on TV. What was the biggest mistake a gunfighter could make? It was forgetting that no matter how fast he was, there was always somebody faster.

It's the same in life. There is always someone smarter or better looking or more tenacious than we are.

Healthy pride—which in no way cancels humility—realizes that personal significance is never achieved by undercutting others. Persons with healthy pride want to establish themselves as viable, respectable individuals, and to that end cooperate with the larger community.

In contrast, false pride is preoccupied with self and inhibits the individual from relating optimally with others. False pride craves control and exhibits an excessive concern with personal preferences and decisions.

Before you wipe your brow and say, "Whew, I'm glad they're not talking about me!" appraise yourself very carefully. Consider the following list of characteristics that indicate false pride. Do any of them look familiar? How does each one imply a potential problem of self-preoccupation?

• Sometimes I nurse critical thoughts too easily.

• I hold onto frustrations longer than necessary.

- Sometimes I simply don't notice the positives in another person's life.

- When something good happens to someone else, I may readily think, *I wish that would happen to me.*

- I get so caught in my own busyness that I can overlook others' needs or feelings.

- I work hard to downplay my negatives; I don't like others to see my weaknesses.

- Sometimes I'll withdraw from people, even when I know it may not be best.

- I get defensive when someone talks with me about improvements I could make.

- Secretly I wish others would handle problems with the same common sense that I use.

- Maintaining a proper image is important to me, even if it means giving others no more than a partial understanding of who I really am.

- In social conversations I interrupt others too easily in mid-sentence.

- I am emphatic in my opinions; others see me as hard-headed.

How did you do? If you identified with none of the statements, you have an even greater problem: denial! Everyone at some point suffers from false pride. By becoming aware of it you can learn how it hurts you and others and what can be done to curtail it.

You learn to put a governor on your raw self-preoccupation as you develop an increasing awareness of the people around you. When you realize that you are not the center of the universe, that people do not exist solely to please you, others will conclude, "Hey, the kid is finally growing up!"

In the maturing process you develop characteristics such as responsibility, fair-mindedness, listening skills, servitude, and concern for others. These are cornerstone traits of humility that also cause you to feel at peace with yourself—in other words, significant!

Sadly, many people never mature in humility. Perhaps a coworker is known for his moodiness or for playing petty power games. Maybe a customer is finicky and manipulative. Perhaps you have friends who major in telling you about their favorite subjects but who are not at all inclined to hear about your items of interest.

Your challenge is to chart your own healthy course without responding to these affronts with your own versions of false pride. Only when your life is characterized by healthy pride do you have an opportunity for true greatness and an opportunity to achieve significance.

A healthy sense of pride runs parallel with humility. It allows you to appreciate your own success or accomplishment, yet without worrying about being noticed. It gives you peace and contentment because it does not force you to look over your shoulder at people you might have hurt in your quest for significance. It propels you toward personal ambitions, yet does not allow you to develop conceited or pompous attitudes.

## Good Managers Are Humble Managers

In consultations with business people, we attempt to strike a balance between building healthy pride and embracing humility.

Good managers take pride in their ability to get things done and to get them done well. They are honest with themselves (humble) and they also seek to let others shine. In other words, they balance pride and humility.

Two types of managers exist in most organizations: Those who look for people less competent than they are so they won't feel threatened; and those who look for people more competent than they are so they can all be successful. The first type is uncertain about personal significance, while the second type finds significance based on the pride/humility balance.

Good managers are often extremely competitive. Many of them have driven personalities. *That also describes a lot of bad managers!* So how can you understand the difference in order to avoid the pitfalls others fall into?

## It's All About Relationships

The real difference between good managers and bad managers is simple. Good managers enjoy good relationships with a wide variety of people; bad managers don't, because they consider relationships a low priority.

And it gets even simpler. Good managers enjoy good relationships with others because they avoid manipulating people to feed their sense of personal significance. Bad managers do just the opposite: They use others in a futile attempt to affirm their own significance.

Consider the true stories of two managers who worked at the same company. One never made a mistake, but his subordinates made a lot. One bored his subordinates with endless stories about himself, while the other would ask those same people about themselves and listen with interest. One spent all of his time talking about his accomplishments; the other spent most of his time talking about the accomplishments of his associates. One was condescending; the other was uplifting. One could not manage anything; the other's staff looked for ways to make him look good.

For which type of manager do you work? Which type of manager are you? And away from work, which type of friend are you? Which kind of spouse? Parent? Neighbor? Are you motivated by humility or false pride? Most importantly, would you be willing to alter your harmful behaviors in order to practice humility?

Weir's Furniture Village of Dallas, Texas, is one of the most successful and highly visible stores of its kind. While Dan Weir is nowhere near ready for retirement, he takes delight in increasingly delegating responsibility for the business to his adult sons and nephews. Most importantly, he is intent on emphasizing the necessity of being a servant both to the buying public and to the store's dozens of employees.

None of these lessons came easy for Dan when he was in his twenties and learning the furniture business from his father. He had not been a standout in school, nor had he kept up with his peers in extracurricular accomplishments. Yet his less-than-stellar beginnings helped him create a management style that has served him well to this day. Those days taught him the utter importance of encouragement.

Two men in particular encouraged him, frequently reminding him of his natural abilities and skills. One of these men, his father-in-law, was a patient listener who openly displayed respect and always found the positive in young Dan's circumstances. The other was a furniture rep who regularly pointed out how talented Dan was and treated him as if he were his most valued account.

As Dan Weir matured and became the key man in the company, he chose to give others what these men had given him. Most companies hand out awards based on achievements, but the Weir company also recognizes employees for character (thoroughness, dependability, resourcefulness, endurance). Not only are these awards given at company meetings, but meritorious works are publicly acknowledged. Often in the Dallas newspaper (with over a million readers), you will find an ad headlined, "At Weir's the Difference Is the People," which features an employee's picture, extolling him or her for unique services or skills. It's all part of a deliberate philosophy to find what is good in people and build upon it.

"The greatest joy I have is encouraging others and seeing them become successful, particularly the underdog," Dan says. He delights in others asking his counsel and advice and knows they feel comfortable in connecting with him because he admits his own failures and mistakes. Is it any wonder that customers and employees show long-term devotion to his company?

Dan's leadership and influence are not built upon ego and control, but upon reassurance and empowerment. That's humility . . . and it is also the foundation for both the receiving and giving of personal significance! "I still struggle with pride," says Dan, yet he determines daily to choose a servant's heart and a learner's spirit. He knows his greatest achievement each day is to build a sense of significance in his people.

Developing humility requires much more than the application of sound techniques. Humility is a state of mind rather than the result of a well-planned scheme for living. It would be no stretch to say that humility arises from a deep sense of mission that assumes your life is a call to service.

## What's Your Mission Statement?

Many organizations develop a mission statement to define their purpose. Some are known for a motto like "A name you can trust" or "We go the extra mile." If you were defined by a mission statement or a motto, what would it be? Look over the following list of potential mottoes. How do you feel about them?

- "I'll milk you for every dollar I can."

- "Power is everything."

- "Who cares about people? Run over anyone who gets in the way."

- "I'm never wrong."

- "Selfishness is life."

- "Be whatever the person in front of you wants you to be."

- "Never offend, only manipulate."

No one would want to be identified with such ideas. Yet as absurd as they are, you probably know someone whose life motto could be so summarized. False pride can grip a person so powerfully that it allows that person to rationalize virtually any way of life.

Now look over the following list of potential mottoes. How do you react to each of these?

- "Service is our middle name."

- "We're not satisfied until you are satisfied."

- "Whatever it takes, we're here for you."

- "Honesty is our policy."

- "We listen to you."

- "Pleasing you pleases me."

- "We'll treat you like one of the family."

Would you be willing to embrace any or all of the above? Millions have and have found they work.

On the other hand, we know some crusty, tough-skinned individuals who would scoff at the notion of setting self's agenda aside in favor of a serving agenda. "That humility business sounds fine in theory," they would say, "but in real life, it gets you nowhere."

Yet they're wrong, and the business world proves it. Humility points to a powerful inner toughness rather than a weak, easily dominated mind-set. Humility recognizes that people deserve goodness. It is committed to being a conduit of the things right and pure. No one ever becomes perfectly humble, yet we believe it is best to aim high rather than to settle for a lower standard.

## Humility May Cost, but It's Worth It

Alex, a dejected sixth grader, made his way to Mrs. Thomas's desk at the front of the room. "I sold sixty-five dollars worth of candy orders for our annual fund-raiser," he explained to the teacher, "but when I reached into my backpack for the money, it was gone. I have the orders that I'm supposed to fill, but I don't know how I'm going to pay for them."

Mrs. Thomas told Alex she'd look into the problem for him. Surely there would be a solution!

Later that day the assistant principal told Mrs. Thomas that if Alex wanted to fill the orders as promised, he'd have to come up with the money. The promotions company would not settle for anything less. As the teacher returned to her classroom, a heavy burden overcame her. She knew Alex to be a solid, reliable kid who didn't lose the money due to irresponsibility. (Later it was discovered to be stolen.) She also knew Alex was poor and could not possibly produce sixty-five dollars.

The next day she told Alex, "I've got good news. The candy company has decided to honor your orders. If it's possible to repay the lost money, then you should do so; but if not, your customers will still get what they bought."

What happened? Mrs. Thomas kept a personal fund of money for emergencies and used that fund to pay for Alex's losses. She did ask Alex to help make up for the lost money with some after-school chores, which he gladly did. But he never knew that Mrs. Thomas had covered for him. She believed in him and felt it was her privilege to assist someone in true need.

We're not suggesting that humble people should dish out money whenever a sad cause comes along, but we do insist that it is good to respond to people at their point of need, even if it involves personal sacrifice. Builders of significance realize their own importance is found in the many ways they can help others.

So ask yourself: What adjustments could you make in order to build a lifestyle founded upon humility? Would you need to ask more questions to learn another's perspective? Would you selflessly pay compliments to others?

As humility increasingly becomes a part of you, you will find your influence expanding. And even if others do not respond to you as your actions deserve, you will still find a peace and contentment you'd never know otherwise.

In the next chapter we will explore how our communication can reflect our commitment to significance building. There is more to interpersonal transactions than is apparent on the surface!

## IT ALL BEGINS WITH YOU

- *Think back about people for whom you have worked. Classify each one as either a "significance builder" or a "significance destroyer."*

- *Look back over the past twenty-four hours. Describe at least two opportunities you had to build the significance of someone else . . . but didn't.*

- *What really good traits do you have that you wish others would recognize?*

- *Who have you known who could be described as a genuinely humble person? What is it about him or her that is so appealing?*

- *False pride can produce short-term power but long-term disloyalty. Who do you know who seems committed to this way of life? When are you most susceptible to this trait?*

- *What restructuring would have to occur for humility to be more central to your character?*

- *In what ways do humility and personal significance overlap?*

# *Chapter* Four
# THE SIGNIFICANCE-BASED TRANSACTION

It was a crowning moment in the minister's career. In his earlier years he had worked diligently, serving his parishioners while also taking doctoral courses at the seminary. Once his reputation was solidly established, he was selected to lead a major church on the East Coast, one of the most coveted positions in his denomination. Located near an internationally known university, the church counted numerous intellectuals as members.

On this day, the minister stood to deliver his homily and was shocked to see a brilliant atheist in attendance, a professor from the university. When the professor continued to come to church Sunday after Sunday, the minister decided he would preach a series of intellectually challenging sermons with the hope of moving the professor to abandon his atheism for the Christian faith. Sure enough, after several weeks, the professor approached the minister.

"I've decided to join your church and renounce my atheism," he said.

"Remarkable!" responded the minister. "Which of my sermons changed your mind?"

"Your sermons?" responded the professor. "Sorry to say, it was not your sermons. One Sunday about three weeks ago, one of your members, a sweet elderly lady, fell in front of the church. I stopped to help her up, and before I knew it she started asking me about my beliefs. She seemed so concerned about me as a person that it caused me to rethink my views. She is the most caring person I've ever met, and I see her tenderness as a reflection of God."

The elderly lady accomplished what the minister could not. While her words were likely not as eloquent as his, she fulfilled the professor's need for spiritual enlightenment by demonstrating to him her belief in his significance.

## Significance-Based Transactions

A "transaction" is any type of communication between two people (whom we might call a sender and a receiver). In a conversation, we frequently change roles. First we send a communication, then we receive a response. Every transaction has at least three elements:

1. What is communicated
2. How it is communicated
3. What is not said, but is communicated

We learn these lessons early in life. Consider the following communication from a parent to a child:

"Jonathan, did you take out the trash?"

Sounds innocent enough, doesn't it? Let's add a little spice to this transaction. We're going to raise the voice of the parent 200 percent in volume. That changes the transaction, doesn't it? Now go even further. Picture the mom, standing there with her hands on her hips (boy, does this bring back childhood memories) and a little redness in her face. "JONATHAN . . . DID YOU TAKE OUT THE TRASH?" We could add one more communication level by showing the mom holding a shredded trash bag in front of a window, trash scattered all over the lawn.

There is so much more to communication than the mere exchange of words! Whether the communication builds significance (the old lady's transaction with the professor) or doesn't (the mom's discussion about the trash), people make lightning-quick interpretations of everything you say and do. To illustrate, take a look at this simple scenario:

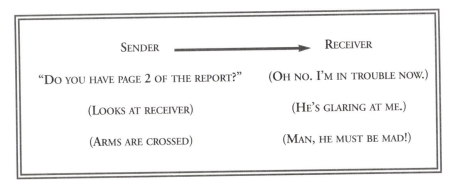

There is more to this transaction than what can be seen on the surface. Was there a problem in the way the receiver interpreted the messages? Or was the sender purposely communicating on two different levels? Notice that the receiver seemed to assume every message was negative. Could it be that the sender had a reputation for being negative? Or was the receiver reading meanings that were not there?

## Levels of Communication

"The problem in our office is that we just don't communicate." Those were the words of a weary mid-level manager, frustrated by the poor information exchange among his colleagues. While his frustration was certainly regrettable and understandable, we would have to conclude that his statement was entirely false!

Why? There is no such thing as *no* communication. Everything you do communicates something. From the look on your face to the pace of your walk to the focus of your eyes, you are sending signals that others receive and interpret. Attitudes and feelings and preferences can be powerfully transmitted even in the absence of words.

Hundreds of times per day you are likely to be involved in some sort of transaction. Your mere presence in someone else's world can begin the process. Every transaction you make, whether it is open and clear or subtle and coded, communicates something about your belief in a person's significance. No transaction, no matter how small, is ultimately devoid of meaning. People add the sum of your messages, looking for trends and tendencies, eventually making assumptions about how you will treat them.

The minister had been unable to influence the atheist professor because they had not yet connected on the deeper levels of communication. The elderly lady, however, succeeded because she used (though not as a ploy) all the elements necessary for a successful transaction. The look on her face must have been magnetic. Her spirit, humble. Her voice, compassionate. Her words, lovingly spoken. Adding the sum of her messages, the professor decided to "buy into" her convictions.

Think for a moment about how you transact with others, with or without words. Are you aware of the impact of your messages? To get an idea of the levels of communication, consider how you might interpret each of the following:

- Several times a day, the same person passes you in the hall, avoiding eye contact and never saying anything.

- A person's foot is tapping throughout a conversation with you.

- A colleague converses with you while staring into the distance, never looking at you.

- You are interrupted frequently while talking about something of interest to you.

- As you are telling a story, the listener stands up when you are about half finished and says, "I don't mean to be rude, but I have to go."

- You place a report on another person's desk and he hardly looks up as he sets it on another pile of documents.

In most of these cases, little was said, but a lot was communicated. In every circumstance, transactions occur. No one can *not* communicate. At the same time, in every transaction you must make a choice: Are you going to make it a positive or a negative communication?

Others (sometimes consciously, sometimes not) are wondering, "What do you think of me? Do you value me? How do I stack up with you? Where do I stand?" Ultimately, the real question is, "Am I important to you? Do I matter?" Your transactions are a constant process in which others are trying to determine how significant they are to you.

We have heard numerous people proudly say, "It doesn't matter to me what people think. I'm my own person and I don't worry about that stuff." While we applaud independent thinking, we would respond to such a statement with a polite but factual "We don't believe that."

The significance principle begins with the assumption that people want and need to feel necessary or important. While some are more thick-skinned than others, even the most ardent independent thinker does care about what others think.

Consider the many people you encounter each day—your spouse, your kids, the boss, coworkers, your customers, even the clerk in the store. You can affect each of these people's significance, either positively or negatively. Are you aware of the mindset that guides your many transactions every day?

As you consider your methods of communication, keep in mind the "iceberg analogy." Only 10 percent of an iceberg is visible, while 90 percent lies below the surface. Most of the ingredients of your communication are hidden from sight, yet they play a vital role in the way you wield your influence. To be most effective in communicating significance, you must be fully aware of the different levels of your transactions.

## Why Communication Breaks Down

Mr. Vickers, an executive of a relatively small business, was perplexed. Speaking to the consultant called in to study company morale, he said, "I'm pretty sure I'm doing things right. I tell my people in staff meetings that they are valuable. I even send out occasional memos explaining how important they are to the company. We've given out an employee-of-the-month certificate for several months in a row. I pay my people a competitive wage. So why do I have such a tremendous turnover in employees?"

As the consultant probed, he found a very different message being received by employees, one that demeaned employee significance. For instance, it was common knowledge that Mr. Vickers was not at all approachable. Though he was never mean-spirited, he was not patient nor did he desire input. Always in a rush, he seemed too busy to be bothered. Furthermore, he was often tense and seemed easily distracted, made poor eye contact, and rarely let anyone finish a thought without jumping in with his own, better idea. At the base of it all, Mr. Vickers seemed to live with the attitude, "I'm the brains of this outfit and don't you forget it."

Even though his spoken words seemed consistent with the significance principle, the rest of his communication was not. This illustrates a key point: *In order to successfully communicate significance, all levels of communication must be consistent with the message you want to send.*

What are those levels? In reverse order of importance, they are:

---

LEVEL 4:   THE SPOKEN WORD, WHAT YOU ACTUALLY SAY.

LEVEL 3:   EMOTIONAL PITCH, SIGNIFYING YOUR APPROACHABILITY.

LEVEL 2:   NONVERBAL CUES, INCLUDING TONE OF VOICE, FACIAL EXPRESSIONS, AND HAND MOVEMENTS.

LEVEL 1:   ATTITUDE, INCLUDING THE DEEPEST BELIEFS THAT DRIVE ALL OTHER BEHAVIOR.

---

Can you see why Mr. Vickers was unsuccessful in communicating significance? While his level 4 communication (spoken words) was good, his level 3 message (emotional pitch) implied tenseness and unapproachability, his level 2 message (nonverbals) suggested he didn't really want to be bothered, and his level

1 message (attitude) strongly communicated that he didn't value people as he said he did.

Do you want to succeed in motivating people? Are you truly committed to the goal of team building and harmonizing? If you are, rather than putting all your energies merely into the top level of communication, start at the foundation.

In the chart below, notice how the four building blocks to successful relationships build upon each other.

**THE FOUR BUILDING BLOCKS TO SUCCESSFUL RELATIONSHIPS**

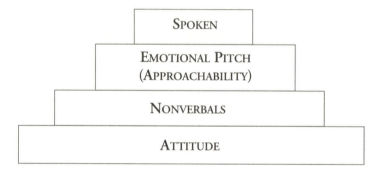

SPOKEN

EMOTIONAL PITCH
(APPROACHABILITY)

NONVERBALS

ATTITUDE

## LEVEL 1: ATTITUDE

A group of psychologists wanted to conduct a study on behavior. They took two little boys to a stable and told each boy they wanted him to go into a "room" for five minutes and then come out and tell the psychologists what he was thinking while in the room. The "room" was actually a horse stall with a lot of manure in it, wired with microphones so the psychologists could listen in on the boys.

As soon as they sent the first boy in, they heard him sighing. In a few moments, the sighs turned into quiet sobs, which almost immediately turned into tears. The team quickly got the child out of the stall.

When they put the second young boy in the room, the outcome was quite different. It wasn't long before he began singing a happy little melody. Soon after that, he began laughing and talking to himself in an excited voice. The psychologists were taken aback by the differences between the two responses, so they asked each boy to explain what he had felt.

The first one told how depressing the stall was. He felt isolated and didn't like being around the horse manure. It quickly got so depressing that he could think only about getting out of there. The other boy explained why he began singing and then laughing by saying, "It didn't take me long to figure out that there had been a pony in that room. I figured that I was going to get a pony just for me, and that got me really excited."

The deepest level of transactions is attitude. Before any verbal or non-verbal communication occurs, your attitudes set the stage. Attitude is the mental filtering system that ultimately determines your thoughts and feelings. As your attitudes repeatedly display themselves, a reputation emerges which ultimately defines you to the world.

Do you have a reputation as an enthusiastic, positive person? If the answer is yes, then you have a head start. Your deeper attitude is revealed in the words you use, such as, "What do you think about this?" or "Since you always do a great job on projects, would you . . . ."

Here's a real nugget for those who want to communicate successfully: If you have a reputation as a positive communicator, *people will listen for the positives in everything you say.* They let their defenses down because they fully believe you are going to say something positive!

The reverse is likewise true. Did you ever watch the popular Saturday night comedy show that featured "Mr. and Mrs. Whiner"?

They said everything in a whining tone. No matter how good something was, they whined about it.

The same is true with people who approach transactions with a negative reputation. People eventually assume negative attitudes are coming. They expect them and even when something positive is said, they try to interpret it in a negative way. It's all about attitude!

Many people have observed that we have become a society of victims. The criminal is the victim of his childhood. The child who acts out at school is the victim of his home life. The slovenly worker is the victim of a bad work environment. The poor person is the victim of an uncaring society. And the list goes on. People will tell you they are victims if you are willing to listen. How often have you heard something like, "If my parents had raised me differently, I would be a brain surgeon today instead of a truck driver"?

But are people truly the victims they claim to be? Or is there a deeper problem with attitude? That was the question posed to a woman we'll call Susan.

Susan Jones could contain herself no longer as she sat in the college class, listening to a discussion about welfare and how the country needed to spend less on those programs. "That's not the truth," she blurted out. "I am one of seven children raised in poverty by a single mother. I got married at age fifteen and had six children. If it weren't for welfare, I wouldn't have the job I have today."

Her professor challenged her with just one statement: "Susan, welfare did not make you the successful administrator you are today . . . you did. You made the decision to take control of your life and you are the one who decided you wanted to live a life of excellence."

After a few minutes of reflection, Susan almost sheepishly looked up and said, "You're right." Susan was a capable, bright person. She could have lived her life in poverty as a capable, bright person. But she chose to live it differently. She chose to maximize every aspect of who Susan Jones is. And she was successful, not because of a program, but because Susan had the character and commitment to accept only the very best for herself.

Incidentally, at last report each of Susan's children were either college graduates or were in college to complete their degrees. Susan obviously gave her children an inheritance of excellence and commitment.

Attitude drives communication and behavior. As you ponder your own attitudes, ask yourself the following questions:

- How much do you care about the success and well-being of others?

- Are your motives kind when you issue directives? Do people sense that you care, even when you confront?

- What is your overall reputation? Fair-minded? Tense? Selfish? Grouchy? Uplifting? Uncertain? Innovative? Enthusiastic?

- Are you more complaint-oriented in your thinking or compliment-oriented?

- Do you believe that most people could succeed if given a fair chance?

- Do you look for what is right, or is it easier for you to spot what is wrong?

## LEVEL 2: NONVERBAL COMMUNICATION

During a field training session, the sales trainer was initially pleased as he watched his protégé give his presentation. The salesman was polite and communicated easily. The client was likewise pleasant and friendly and she seemed interested in his product.

When the salesman needed to show the client a picture, he stepped eagerly to her side and stood near her . . . much too near. She immediately leaned back slightly and lowered her head. Unaware of his overwhelming presence, the salesman continued. She continued to lean away from him as he continued moving closer. As the woman lowered herself toward the table top, she had to prop herself up by putting one arm on the side of her head. Undaunted, he continued until her head was resting on the table, covered by her arm. She had long since quit listening to his words. She wanted only separation!

Nonverbal communication can be much more powerful than what you say. Your nonverbals can communicate a deep respect for others, just as they can speak of disrespect. They signal your level of interest, your willingness to be patient, your degree of confidence, or your lack of these traits.

Picture yourself in a familiar setting, perhaps in your company's conference room or your neighbor's yard or a customer's office or the place your companions hang out for lunch. Are you there? Now observe your tendencies. Beyond your spoken words, what messages would the other persons around you be perceiving? Look over the following list of nonverbal cues and identify what your natural tendencies are:

- Facial expression: interested or bored?

- Focus of the eyes: tuned in or tuned out?

*People will listen for the positives in everything you say.*

- Hand gestures: eager or detached?

- Voice animation: optimistic or critical?

- Pace of speech: confident or unsure?

- Position of your body: engaged or ready to leave?

- Manner of listening: understanding or interrupting?

Probably you have heard the expression "What you say is not as important as how you say it." It is true. A psychiatrist friend hosted a radio call-in show for years. When he meets his listening public at seminars and speeches, he will occasionally hear, "You sure do give sound advice." But far more often he will hear, "When I listen to you on the radio, you seem so genuinely interested and kind; you have no idea how helpful that is to me."

In your world, people also look to you for cues to determine if they matter. While you may memorize and speak wonderful words, they will get no further than where your nonverbals will take them. Because nonverbals tend to be more closely aligned to your true subconscious thoughts, people in your world will believe your cues far more readily than your consciously monitored words.

## LEVEL 3: EMOTIONAL PITCH

As you transmit your attitudes and nonverbal cues, you take on an emotional pitch that greatly influences the way your message is received. Remember, the significance principle states that all people are driven by the desire to be accepted or to be necessary. Therefore men and women in your world are constantly assessing whether you value or devalue them.

You do the same thing when you listen to public speakers. Inevitably you weigh their emotional pitch to determine if you can trust their words. If you hear a person tell a funny story at a banquet, you might immediately think, *I like the guy and I want to hear more.* But if that same person jokes and cuts up while delivering a eulogy, you would think, *Get this terribly inappropriate person out of here.*

Which emotional elements are most necessary in communicating significance? Look over the following list of contrasts and identify which one in each pair you would rather encounter:

- Contentment or dissatisfaction
- Warmth or aloofness
- Calm firmness or aggressive anger
- Interest or indifference
- Confidence or insecurity
- Friendliness or rejection
- Equality or superiority
- Approachable or impossible to read

It's not a hard choice, is it? Emotional tone makes a world of difference in communicating significance. Just look at the life of Jackie Birdwell.

If you spent much time in the last thirty years at the Baylor University malt and hamburger shop in the student union building, you know Jackie Birdwell. Well into middle age (he guards his years carefully), Jackie has become a legend to those who have made his acquaintance.

Short and stocky, with closely cropped hair and a picket-fence smile, Jackie's work days follow the same routine. He rises from his one-room apartment at a local boarding house and walks a few blocks to "The Bear" where he goes to work, filling food orders for university students and faculty. Quiet and down to business, Jackie prides himself in his reliability. The shop's regulars call to him by name, and in most cases he can respond in kind.

Jackie summarizes his life simply. "I've been here a real long time," he says. "Sometimes things don't go my way. Sometimes I have bad days and sometimes I have good days, but it's just one of those things. I like my job, I've met a lot of people, and they come back to see me."

Often Jackie's work will be interrupted when he sees one of his favorites. He'll stop what he's doing, go around the counter to give the person a big hug, then with his hand on the person's shoulder, he'll say with great kindness, "I've been missing you." Reared with his only brother at a children's home in the 1950s and '60s, placed in special education courses through those years, Jackie will never be accused of being academically overstimulated. Yet what he may lack in intellect, he more than makes up in spirit. His emotional pitch says, "When you're in my presence, it's safe. I'm safe."

Through the years Jackie has been honored in many ways. Prominent student groups have given him memberships in their organizations. The football team has adopted him as their number one fan, and he has befriended many of the high profile young men. The Methodist Home where he was reared has honored him as an outstanding alumnus, the youngest ever so honored. The Texas Association for Retarded Citizens gave him the title of "Statewide Employee of the Year." The school's student congress cited him for distinguished service to the university. And to top it all off, he sings in the choir at the church he has belonged to for decades.

Jackie's magical way with people has virtually nothing to do with articulate words or a polished manner. In fact, if he tried to speak eloquently, he'd be much less believable. Jackie touches people at an emotional level that makes them feel warm and accepted. With his simple, unpretentious nature he projects a calm, pleasant demeanor that causes people to come back for more.

Would you aspire to be a Jackie Birdwell? Builders of significance know the value of setting the right emotional atmosphere with one key trait: approachability. Rather than overwhelming others with a critical spirit or losing influence with an insincere demeanor, they project a message of concern and optimism. As one appreciative employee told his manager, "You may not always agree with me. You may even be disappointed in me. But somehow I know that you believe in me and want the best for me." Is it any wonder this manager inspires tremendous loyalty in his workers?

## LEVEL 4: SPOKEN WORDS

While your attitude, nonverbal cues, and emotional pitch set the stage for your ability to communicate significance, the words you speak are the finishing touch. Remember the phrase, "Sticks and stones may break my bones but words will never harm me"? Whoever coined that phrase must have lived on a different planet!

A school administrator once said to a consultant, "I hope you're not going to tell me I'm supposed to say syrupy, sweet words to my faculty, because I'm just not that kind of person. I like to tell it like it is!" There's no problem in telling it like it is and you certainly don't have to be syrupy sweet to communicate positive truths; yet the words you choose are very important. They determine much of your success with people.

An administrative assistant, Amy, walked into the office of her boss with a letter of resignation. Stunned, the boss asked why she was quitting. With futility in her voice she responded, "I want to work where I'm appreciated, plain and simple."

The boss dropped his jaw. "You've got to be kidding!" he exclaimed. "You're very valuable to my work here and I appreciate you greatly. I thought you knew that."

Amy's response was calm and to the point. "I've been here five years and I cannot recall one compliment," she said, "but if I had a dollar for every complaint I've heard, I'd probably be a millionaire."

Sound familiar? Some people have an inordinately difficult time saying words like:

- "You're very valuable to me."

- "I love you."

- "Let me tell you what is right about you."

- "I'm so proud you're on my team."

- "I enjoy working next to you."

Once you align your attitudes, nonverbal cues, and emotional pitch with the significance principle, you can complete the communication with well-chosen words. People usually respond to sincerely spoken words of encouragement.

Steve Grissom heads Divorce Care, a nationwide organization based in Raleigh, North Carolina, that helps in the healing of those injured by divorce. His nonprofit organization distributes its own videos and written materials to groups (mostly churches) that help those in need.

Steve's case is unusual because he had no background in this type of work. He trained as a journalist and for thirteen years before beginning his new career, he served as a vice president for a communications company specializing in satellite technology.

The word *confident* does not describe him in those early stages of putting together Divorce Care. Steve readily admits to feelings of uncertainty and doubt.

How did he overcome this lack of confidence? Words. Though a confident person by nature, Steve needed someone to say, "I believe in you." His wife, Cheryl, could easily have said, "Stick to a business that's familiar; why tamper with success?" But she did not; she chose to speak words of encouragement. Steve's minister could have said, "Dealing with the freshly divorced will wear you out. Why not consider an easier way of life?" But he, too, was free with words of support. Close friends could have said, "You're crazy," but instead they responded with enthusiasm. Steve looks back to the many hours one friend, Dave Williams, spent with him during those formative days. "I am still amazed at how much time he invested in me," he says.

The Divorce Care program now has six thousand locations across the country, wildly surpassing the most optimistic projections. New healing programs are in the works and people are being genuinely helped.

What might have happened if the key people in Steve Grissom's life had spoken discouragement and doubt? How many thousands of people would already have been deprived if Steve had heard only from his detractors and agreed, "You're probably right"?

People weigh carefully what you say and what you believe. Spoken words represent a form of commitment to the thoughts and attitudes that might otherwise remain hidden. Significance builders put their words out in the open, committing themselves to encourage and uplift their hearers by what they say.

In your place of business, who needs words of edification? How would your sphere of influence broaden if you regularly spoke compliments?

One executive we know heard some especially encouraging compliments from a client regarding the way his new assistant had handled a delicate problem. After concluding that conversation, he asked his assistant to stop into his office for a moment. *Oh no*, she immediately thought, *What have I done wrong?* She took a seat in front of his massive desk as he spoke. "I just got off the phone with Mr. Harris," he explained, "and he told me how he appreciated your handling of the problem he discussed with you. I want you to know how pleased I am to hear such glowing reports from a valued client. You have represented me and the company quite well and I thought you would like to know about the nice things being said about you behind your back."

How do you suppose the executive's words registered in the assistant's mind? How would *you* have felt if you were the assistant?

Words. People gravitate toward those who speak uplifting words. Do you have a reputation for this?

### CHECKING YOUR BUILDING BLOCKS OF COMMUNICATION

- *How do you think your coworkers would describe your attitude?*

- *What words best describe the emotional pitch of your conversations?*

- *What nonverbals characterize your communication with others?*

- *How would your friends describe the words you use to communicate with them?*

## *Chapter* Five
# TRANSACTIONS THAT TRANSFORM

If you asked most police officer trainees to name the most difficult part of their training, you might be surprised at their answer. Their biggest challenge is not always in what they have to learn, but rather what they have to unlearn.

As firearms instructor Steve Campbell begins his instruction for the one-week course, students are told to take their unloaded weapons and lay them on the desk. After checking the guns to ensure they are unloaded, Campbell proceeds with the lesson. Students are told to put on their holsters and insert the pistols into the holsters. Then they are told to draw their weapons and point at an imaginary target.

"Look at that!" roars Campbell. "Every one of you is breaking standard police procedure!" As the confused police cadets try to figure out the problem, Campbell makes his point. "The most difficult thing a new police officer has to learn is to draw his weapon *without putting his finger on the trigger.*" Most of us learned from westerns that you draw your gun with your finger on the trigger. It's so automatic we do it without thinking.

People who teach new skills insist that their most difficult teaching is with students who already "know" something about that skill. According to most instructors, teaching people to change something they have done all their life consumes inordinate amounts of time and energy. That is why most teaching professionals like to start with young children who have not yet been introduced to the subject.

"Here's your homework for every night this week," the gruff voice of Campbell continues. "I want you to go home and put on your gun and stand in front of a full-length mirror. Each time you draw, make sure your trigger finger is aligned straight down the side of the gun, off of the trigger. Now, some of you will be tempted to give up on this, especially after the first night of practice. Here's what you do. You practice 200 draws every night for a week, and by the end of the week you will be on your way to a new habit."

At the end of a week of such homework, the students were amazed. They actually *could* draw without putting their fingers on the trigger. More amazing yet, by the end of the week, most of them didn't even have to think about it. It had become automatic.

Officer Campbell demonstrated that no matter how ingrained a behavior is, *it is possible to change*. Change, even difficult change, can be one of the most rewarding challenges we face.

Officer Campbell (now a former police chief) called his approach "muscle memory." The idea is that if you repeat something enough, it becomes rote. In the same way, changing transactions requires a concerted effort to stop and adjust communication styles.

Have you ever known anyone who lost fifty pounds, then gained it all back within a few months? Most of us have either done something like this or known someone who endured a similar struggle. For those who struggle with dieting, keeping weight off involves learning how to eat well. The problem with people who lose weight and gain it all back is that they never changed their dietary habits. So when they went off the diet, they gained back all of their weight. Recent research has indicated that most people who go on a diet find that weight loss is temporary at best.

## Transactional Modeling

Many think change is merely a matter of will power. It involves the will, yet it is more. It requires an understanding of how to gradually change our habits from unhealthy to healthy. And the key to behavioral change is transactional modeling (TM).

What makes TM so powerful is that it allows you to focus upon one thing at a time. In that way, change becomes much more manageable. Here is the basic approach to TM:

1. Identify the transaction you would like to change.
2. Evaluate a "desired" vs. "undesired" response.
3. Focus upon the desired response.
4. Force the desired response.

Think your way through a simple issue in your life you would like to change. For instance, do you have a problem with interrupting people before they are finished speaking? Apply the transactional model to change that behavior, something like this:

1. Joan is talking; this is when I sometimes interrupt.
2. The best thing for me to do is to wait until I'm sure she's finished.
3. I will listen carefully as I concentrate on patience.
4. I will choose to let Joan finish her train of thought.

Consider another typical situation. You always get into political arguments with someone you see approaching you. "Well, if isn't that yukko liberal," says Bob. "What's your jerk president done to mess up America this week?"

Your transactional model:

1. Here comes Bob again. This is how we get into arguments.
2. The best thing for me to do is to find a way to ask him a positive question.
3. Ohhh, he makes me mad! I'm going to think up something positive instead of getting angry.
4. (This hurts) "Bob, what do you think about the balanced budget idea?"

How did it work? Not entirely painless? Not entirely successful? But the question is, *was it an improvement?* Our guess is, yes. And it will get better with practice.

## "I Want You to Change Just One Thing"

John was classified as one of the best tennis teachers around, so good that internationally ranked professionals signed up for lessons. John was a unique teacher with an innate ability to take students to levels of performance they never thought they would reach. What was so unique about John?

Tennis can be complex, which means adjusting someone's tennis game can be complex. The challenge is to break through habits the student has developed over years of play and to move the student past those performance-inhibitors. More often than not, the student doesn't have one large problem; likely there are many small problems. A trained professional might look at a player and conclude seven key issues must be changed if the student is to correct the problems. That can be confusing to the student, and that's where John's approach is so valuable.

"I want you to change just one thing." That is how John started out each lesson. For the next thirty minutes, he put the student through various drills focusing on only one aspect of her game. He might hit for that entire time with her, concentrating only upon the weight shift from her back foot to her front foot as she hits the ball. Once she got it down, John would say, "I want you to do just one more thing. I want you to point your shoulder at the ball when you hit a backhand." Little did the student realize that as she concentrated on pointing her shoulder on the backhand, her weight shift was perfect. Why was it perfect? Because she had "modeled the transaction" so many times that now she did it without even thinking. John's students became excellent tennis players one transaction at a time.

A manager in a meeting recently said, "I manage thirty people. How can I think about this TM stuff with thirty people?"

"With how many people on your team do you have serious problems?" we asked.

"Only about two," she replied. We then reminded her that she dealt only with one person at a time. Further, all she really had to focus on was one transaction at a time.

Focusing on one transaction at a time. That is what makes it possible to change the way you respond to others and the way you treat people. You can most effectively change your behavior by attending to just one issue at a time.

Melissa, a manager, was challenged to identify five communication problems she might have in dealing with Fred, a problem employee. After a lot of thought, she made the following list of what she did:

- Fume when he turned in sloppy work.

- Talk about him behind his back to other employees.

- Gripe about how he needed to come up to standard.

- Speak disrespectfully to him when discussing his work.

- Approach him pessimistically when evaluating his work.

For Melissa, it took a lot of honest self-examination to admit what she was doing. But only after she identified the elements that fed her unsuccessful transactions was she able to make progress. Prior to the exercise she had focused upon how to "fix Fred." As a result of the exercise, she focused upon something more substantial—she concluded that she was allowing Fred's bad attitude to affect how she approached him. She decided it would be more productive to deal with him in a proactive, positive manner, regardless of his attitude.

## A Sample Conversation

Listen in to the following conversation between Sam and Susan. Sam is a taker and Susan is a giver. But notice how she chooses to sustain her own healthy agenda rather than getting caught in Sam's self-promoting transaction:

Sam: Guess what? I just learned who the top sales award is going to!

Susan: Who, Sam?

Sam: Why, none other than me—the best salesman in the division.

Susan: That's great, Sam. Did you notice that Belinda had the highest sales increase award? You both should be congratulated.

*For as he thinketh in his heart, so he is.  Proberbs 23:7*

Sam seeks out an audience so he can brag about all the great things he is doing. Susan, a really good listener, was tired of Sam's "taking" all of the time, but notice how she began establishing a way to positively change her transactions with Sam.

Susan could have insulted Sam by pointing out that Belinda was number one in another area, but by responding to him as she did, she sent him two very clear messages: First, you are significant; second, you are not the only significant individual around. From a practical standpoint, Susan was using transactional modeling not only to change her behavior, but to positively change a painful transactional pattern with Sam.

Have you ever dealt with someone like Sam? It isn't natural to say something nice about him, knowing his usual arrogant, self-serving behavior, is it? For most of us that would be difficult. Many of us have tried what Susan did, only to lose out later in the conversation. We must keep in mind two keys to learning how to use the significance principle in developing positive communications:

1. *It takes time.* Be patient! The longer you model positive responses, the easier it gets.
2. *It takes practice.* Once you get the hang of using the TM-significance approach, you can begin linking a number of transactions into an entire conversation.

## TM Applied: The LIFT Model

We were recently asked to work on developing a sales training program. Early in our discussions, we expressed concern with sales programs that offer "157 Keys to Effective Selling" or something similar. We insisted that behavioral change approaches must be succinct if they are to be effective. Just like the tennis student who cannot change seven major aspects of his game simultaneously, the person seeking to become a builder of significance has to be able to break learning into small, understandable bites. We developed the LIFT approach as a way to succinctly describe how communication adjustments can be most effectively managed.

# LIFT

1. **Listen** *carefully to understand what is being communicated. Listening is the key to developing effective responses. Listening helps you identify the significance-based aspects of the message.*

2. **Identify** *the two possible responses (significance building/significance destroying) that you might choose. It is important to remember that our need for significance often tempts us to choose the response that builds our own significance at the expense of others.*

3. **Force** *the appropriate response. Good relationships are a choice. We must force ourselves to choose the response that enables us to build bridges, not barriers, to positive relationships.*

4. **Target** *significance-building transactions. No matter how abrasively a conversation may begin, you can turn it into a positive transaction. Your ability to target and maintain your focus upon significance issues is the key to success.*

## LISTEN

Who do you know that refuses to listen when you are talking? Have you ever known someone who tried to suggest you were saying the exact opposite of what you were actually communicating? The problem is these individuals never learned how to listen.

An international company discovered that one of the biggest problems facing its sales force was an inability to listen. The answer? Training the salespeople in the art of listening. Listening was the key to the company's sales success.

If you want growing, positive relationships, the key to success is your ability to listen. How do you learn this skill? Use the "Four Building Blocks of Communication" to develop your listening skills.

*Attitude:* Early in the conversation you will begin to understand the attitude of the person you are dealing with. You might say he is "negative" or "positive" or "enthusiastic," but generally you will find you can quickly identify the person's basic attitude.

*Nonverbals:* As you enter a conversation, you will often observe a person's arms crossed or her body turned away from you. You learned early in life that a person's eyes send a lot of messages. All of these "keys" work together to help you understand the real message of the person you are talking with.

Law enforcement professionals learned long ago that nonverbals can reveal whether a person is telling the truth. A seasoned interrogator is often able to challenge a subject's statements after only a few minutes of conversation. Some interrogators are so good that they rarely, if ever, err in detecting a lie.

*Emotional Pitch:* Anger, assertiveness, weakness, rage, or vulnerability are just a few of the emotions you might detect early in a conversation. Many times the words will be almost pleasant, but certain emotional keys will signal a very different message.

*The Spoken Word:* Spoken words offer us two opportunities to understand a given communication. While a person uses words to communicate his message, certain words reveal a great deal more about what they mean. For instance, the use of imperatives like "must" or "should" often suggests the real message. In the next chapter ("Anger in the Workplace") we will offer a more detailed explanation of these issues.

Most of us have noticed a "funny feeling" inside when talking with someone. Bankers often say that before making a bad loan, they had this "funny inside feeling" every time. No doubt you have had the same experience. Something makes you suspicious about someone, even though everything on the exterior appears normal. Often you discover that you should have paid attention to those feelings.

What was going on to produce those odd feelings? Usually it's the nonverbals—emotional pitch, attitude, body language—that sets off the alarms. You already know you should probably listen to those alarms, but we are suggesting you go one step further: Listen to conversations with the four building blocks of communication in mind so that you understand the real message.

## IDENTIFY

A lot of communication involves emotion, which contradicts the idea that the real objective in communication is to transfer information from one party to another. As you manage the four building blocks of communication, you deal with both the facts of the communication and the emotion of the communication.

Since communication involves emotion, the possibility of responding emotionally is great. If someone speaks to you in an angry manner, for instance, you may be tempted to give an angry reply.

If you want to communicate in ways that build relationships, it is important to be aware of this tendency to respond emotionally. Instead, we must replace the response with one that avoids the emotional traps and pitfalls that defeat the goal of creating a positive relationship.

That means you have to identify both possible responses: The (negative) emotional response and the (positive) significance-enhancing response. Without conscious effort we will almost always respond emotionally, so the key is to quickly look at both responses and tell ourselves which is positive and which is negative. By identifying the two responses, we are able to begin changing our basic patterns of communication.

## FORCE

"Force might sound a little threatening, but it really isn't. Have you ever told someone to "bite your lip" before he said something he did not want to say? You wanted the person to stop long enough to avoid the negative response, thus allowing his better judgment to lead toward a positive response.

Forcing is merely choosing to do that which builds positive relationships. If you are like most people, you wish you could change some aspects of the way you communicate. Maybe sometimes you feel like the comedian Flip Wilson, whose favorite line was, "The devil made me do it." Forcing the positive response means that you intend to change your relationships, one transaction at a time. It also means that you commit to "take your stand" by making the basic changes that change the way you conduct yourself.

## TARGET

Goal setting works. By targeting significance-building transactions, you can maintain the course toward change. Without a set goal, you can wander far afield—as any sailor could tell you.

Many people fall in love with sailing the moment they board a sailboat, but while it can be a peaceful and relaxing pastime, it can also be frustrating for captain and crew if the person steering the boat fails to understand one of the basics: Steer a straight course. New sailors learn to sail toward a fixed point or landmark, freeing the crew from constantly adjusting sails and rigging.

The same is true for learning to enjoy positive relationships: You must steer a straight course. By targeting significance-building transactions as your "fixed point," you can focus upon the goal that creates truly positive relationships.

## Changing Our Relationships

The advent of faster, more powerful airplanes during World War II created new problems for pilots. Aircraft like the P-51 fighter were able to approach the speed of sound by entering a steep dive. Aviation designers had long been interested in what happened when an airplane closed in on the speed of sound.

One shocking discovery was that under certain conditions, the controls of an aircraft would "reverse out." This meant the pilot needed to move the controls opposite the usual direction. In a number of cases, "reverse out" resulted in crashes. Even when a pilot knew of his aircraft's tendency to reverse out in a steep dive, it was extremely difficult to get him to do the opposite of his training.

So how did the Air Force approach this problem? First, pilots were given practice in identifying the conditions under which the controls reversed out. Next, they worked with an experienced pilot who led them through a flight maneuver involving this problem. Finally, they executed the maneuver themselves.

Achieving personal change happens much the same way. We must first learn to recognize the circumstances that necessitate a change. We must then choose the significance-building approach in favor of the emotional response. Finally, we must make this a permanent practice. It must become a part of how we build relationships.

What personal habits hinder you from achieving this goal? Are you known as a critic? Are you so driven that you blow right past people? Or are you passive or disinterested? A poor or impatient listener?

It's okay to admit where you go astray; we all need mid-course corrections. There is no shame in that, *as long as we make the necessary adjustments.* Right now, your task is to target the specific behaviors that you intend to alter, then look for opportunities to begin the change.

May we make a major suggestion as you focus your energy on change? Make yourself accountable to someone, whether it be a spouse or a friend or a coworker. Tell that person about your new plans and intentions and ask him or her to talk with you about your progress. By openly declaring your intentions, your efforts are bound to be more diligent. Rather than merely *thinking* about change, you will actually find yourself changing!

Of course, change is rarely a problem-free process. Conflict and tension can pull you back into unhelpful patterns. In the next chapter we will explore how you can favorably handle your reactions to conflict so you can stay on course toward becoming a builder of significance.

## TRANSACTIONAL MODELING: A PERSONAL ASSESSMENT

- *Identify two or three relationships in which your ability to respond differently could positively change those relationships.*

- *What two or three interpersonal "habits" would you like to change?*

- *When you look back at past problems in work or social settings, what interpersonal "significance" issues might have contributed to the problems?*

- *Think of a friend who has problems with relationships. If he or she asked you how they could enjoy better relationships, what would you say?*

- *What commitments do you need to make to positively change your own relationships?*

- *If you were able to make some of the changes you listed above, what do you think would happen to your relationships?*

- *How could transactional modeling be used in your work setting to improve your interpersonal skills or to help others change theirs?*

# *Chapter* Six
# ANGER IN THE WORKPLACE

Imagine yourself driving home from a hectic day at work. As you approach a busy intersection you encounter a red light. What do you do? Of course, you obey the signal and stop. You continue driving when a flashing light on your car's control panel begins to blink. You're low on oil. Now what? You heed the signal and stop by the lube shop. When you get home you turn on the light and the bulb blows. Another signal—time to change the light-bulb. You pop some food into the microwave and in minutes you hear a beep, the signal that tells you the food is ready.

Get the idea? Daily you respond to signals that guide you toward a more orderly, functional way of life. Without signals, chaos and confusion result.

A major signal in the human personality indicates when personal significance is jeopardized. Over and over each day it goes off, hoping to prompt you to do something to get life on the right track. That signal is your anger.

When you regularly feel anger, one of two possibilities is being signaled:

1. You are not sufficiently aware of the significance needs of those around you (and are probably trying to advance your own agenda even if it means you hurt others);

2. You are feeling insignificant because someone else is not responding to your legitimate needs.

Whether it flares at work, at home, among friends, or with extended family members, anger is a signal that says, "Someone is failing to recognize the need for significance."

What picture comes to mind when you think about an angry person? Perhaps you imagine a person with a drawn facial expression, a fiery look in the eyes, speaking loud and sharp words, forceful in character. That would certainly picture anger . . . yet it would not be a very full picture. Anger is not a one-dimensional emotion. Just as personalities vary widely, so is anger expressed in many ways.

Often we will hear someone say, "I don't get angry very often, but I do feel frustrated a good bit." What such a person really means is, "When I get angry, I don't necessarily shout and scream." Frustration is merely a muffled form of anger. Anger may also be disguised as impatience, annoyance, irritability, a critical spirit, disillusionment, and punishing withdrawal. While anger may provoke loud and unruly behavior, it may just as easily stimulate some quiet, behind-the-scenes expression of agitation.

Your quest to live with a full sense of significance will be incomplete without understanding the anger and tension that you and those in your world may experience. The question is, how can it be managed in a way that keeps significance alive?

# How to Respond to Anger

## DEFINE YOUR ANGER

The first step in responding to anger is to understand its function. Think of the moments you do not feel angry (or frustrated or impatient or annoyed). Anger is not present when people are cooperative, helpful, encouraging, kind, understanding, or attentive. In the presence of those qualities you are likely to feel content and significant.

Anger is provoked by noncooperation, unhelpfulness, criticism, a mean spirit, poor understanding, inattentiveness. Your anger is spurred by the thought that you deserve better. Your significance is being invalidated and you want the provocation to cease.

Anger can thus be defined as the emotion of self-preservation. Anger is directly linked to the desire to be understood as significant. Through anger you demonstrate your desire to preserve one of three issues:

1.  Your innate sense of worth
2.  The legitimacy of your needs
3.  Your foundational convictions

Let's get an idea of how to understand anger's link to significance by examining a mid-level executive we'll call Steve. This man is well educated and has been in the research and development department of a software products company for the past four years. When he was hired, Steve was told he was going to be a valuable asset to the company; executives prized a keen, inquisitive mind like his.

But Steve's four years with the company did not bear out those glowing words. From the very beginning, Steve was paired with

Harry, a man who was less than humble. Harry was always right and anyone who disagreed with him quickly heard just how superior Harry was. He showed no flexibility and you learned that to keep peace you kept quiet and tried not to upset Harry.

Steve, a withdrawn and mellow man, was not a combative person. In meetings with Harry he usually found himself on the losing end of discussions. On a few occasions Steve attempted to discuss his conflicts with Harry, but he never got too far. He also tried to discuss the problem with their immediate supervisor, Liz, but she said, "I'm not getting in the middle. Work it out between yourselves."

One Thursday afternoon after a divisional meeting dominated by Harry, Steve silently returned to his desk, picked up his jacket and keys, and left the building without saying a word to anyone. The next morning when he failed to appear at his desk, Liz called him at home. "For four years I've been taking bull from that man next to me," Steve said. "My ideas have been summarily dismissed and I've been told if I can't get along with him, it's just my problem. On several occasions I've tried to talk with people who would be in a position to help, but it's gotten me absolutely nowhere. If you people want me to work at your company, that's fine, but it will be on one condition: Do something about that jerk!" Then in an uncharacteristic move, he slammed down the phone.

Clearly Steve was nursing anger, though no one knew just how strong it was until he blew up. What was at the core of his emotion? First, Steve was taking a stand of self-preservation. For four years he had felt invalidated; he would take it no more. In anger he was preserving:

1. His personal worth. "It's time someone showed me some respect."

2. His legitimate needs. "I need to feel like my input will be considered seriously."
3. His foundational convictions. "Dominant personalities should not be allowed to bully others."

Was his emotion legitimate? Absolutely. Like most people who get angry, Steve had some legitimate concerns. Did he handle his anger productively? Well, that's another story. Steve had suppressed his anger many times, and finally when he spoke up, he communicated aggressively.

In Steve's defense, we might add that the office milieu did not encourage him to fairly process his emotions. Nonetheless, his anger got the best of him. He felt as if his significance had been robbed and as emotion welled up inside, he chose to communicate in a way that invalidated the significance of someone else. In this case it was Liz.

Regardless of the type of environment you work in, you will inevitably experience anger in some form. A coworker will fail to follow through on an assignment. You may be ignored. Someone may act rudely toward you. You may be unfairly criticized. In short, anger cannot be dodged. Like Steve, you'll have to decide what you will do once anger is present.

In order to keep your significance intact while also building the significance of others, you must have a good idea of what to do with anger. While it is impossible to determine when and where your anger will appear, once you are aware of its presence, you can learn to make choices consistent with the significance principle.

First, understand that there is both unhealthy and healthy anger. The key difference between the two is that one robs persons of their significance while the other does not. At its origin, most anger can be described as neutral; it is tied to a desire to preserve worth, needs, and convictions. Your use of it determines if the anger becomes healthy or not.

Suppose you are asked to help on a project at work. Your job is to gather information, then distribute your findings to several others who need the input to complete a report for a crucial customer. When you ask an associate for help, she cheerfully says she'll be glad to assist you . . . then proceeds to ignore you for two days. You attempt to check on the status of her work and she won't return your calls. Finally you trap her in the hallway and she gives you a brush-off, indicating you're just wasting your time.

Meanwhile, you put together the best information you can and give it to your divisional supervisor. As he scans the material he immediately begins griping, but this doesn't surprise you since he is known as a grouch. He complains that you omitted some key information and you retort that this customer doesn't want the information the supervisor says you should have. Not listening, he insists that you rewrite the report and have it on his desk tomorrow. You know, of course, that you have at least three days of legwork to do to meet his requirements.

Stop here. What are you feeling? Tense? Agitated? Unappreciated? Ignored? These are all expressions of anger. Is the emotion legitimate? Yes! You've been ignored, even betrayed by your associate, then misunderstood and belittled by the boss. It makes sense that you are angry. In your frustration you wish to preserve your worth, needs, and convictions. You want to feel significant to these two people.

It is at this point that you are forced to choose. Which direction will your anger take you, healthy or unhealthy? Toward being a significance builder or destroyer?

*The outcome of anger is personal defeat. Our ability to succeed is proportional to our ability to deal first with our own anger issues.*

## UNHEALTHY ANGER

If you want, you can choose one of three unhealthy options. It may seem silly to think that anyone would deliberately choose an unhealthy path, but keep in mind that when we mismanage anger, it is indeed the result of a choice. Let's look at the three unhealthy options. How common are they in your life?

1) *Suppressing anger.* Some people hate to admit anger in their personalities. Usually they have been taught that anger is wrong, or at least that anger results in increased conflict and pain. So to avoid prolonged unpleasantness, they reason it would be safer to pretend their anger does not exist. For instance, in your hypothetical work project you might say to the boss's unreasonable request, "You know I'll do what I can to get it to you tomorrow." Inside you may be seething, but he'll never know.

Do you ever choose to suppress your anger? Look at the following behaviors, identifying which ones might be common for you:

- You say yes when you really need to say no.

- You take on more than you know you can handle.

- It is important to keep a "good guy" reputation, even if it requires giving false impressions.

- If someone asks, "How's it going?" you'll say "Okay," even though it's not.

- When you have a legitimate complaint, you hold it inside as you remind yourself that you don't want to create trouble.

- You hesitate to ask for help or express a need, even when it is warranted.

- You are a conflict avoider.

Do any of these behaviors describe you? If so, you are sitting on your own emotional powder keg. You are likely to regularly experience stress or discouragement or demotivation or depression. The anger you hold inside is wearing you out, leaving you longing for relief.

Notice how the suppression of your legitimate anger runs counter to your need for significance. By choosing to stuff your anger you demean your own worth, needs, and convictions, and insinuate that your personal value does not warrant attention. Do you really believe that?

2) *Aggressive expressions of anger.* Some people leave little room for doubt that they're angry. They are bold and public when they feel their significance is being denied. Anger grips their personalities and takes over their behavior. The emotion may be legitimate, yet it is communicated in a way that demeans or intimidates others.

Go back to your hypothetical work situation. Instead of smiling as you leave your boss's office, you openly complain, "You never give me enough time to complete a project. What's the deal around this place . . . do you think we're slaves?" And when you encounter the noncooperative associate you might growl, "If you'd spend less time on the phone and more time concentrating on important matters, you wouldn't always be late with your work." You are preserving your worth, needs, and convictions . . . but at someone else's expense.

Look over the following list of traits to determine if any aggressive anger traits are common to you:

- You speak bluntly without regard for the other's dignity.

- You are known for being opinionated, even inflexible.

- As you take care of your own needs you do not necessarily factor in others' needs as well.

- You can be argumentative.

- Behind your back people say you don't listen.

- You speak critical, negative words with relative ease.

- Your goal in disagreements is to be more convincing than the other person.

Aggressive anger is shortsighted. It charges head-on into the problem, and may even achieve immediate results, but in the grand scheme it generates poor returns. A receiver with a sour taste in his mouth is not so likely to budge the next time.

Aggressive anger inhibits significance-building communication because it places others in a position of inferiority. The nonverbal cues accompanying aggression imply a sense of disregard and disdain for the other person. Aggression is indeed a choice . . . but a poor one.

3) *Passive-aggressive anger.* Some people feel the need to vent their frustrations in nonedifying ways, yet they do not want to be fully accountable for their anger. These people often choose passive-aggressive means of handling conflict. They attempt to preserve personal worth, needs, and convictions at someone else's expense, while drawing the least amount of attention to the depth of their angry feelings.

Return once more to our hypothetical situation. The boss tells you the report is due tomorrow, thereby making you angry. As you leave his office, you tell him you'll get it done; but tomorrow, when he asks for it, you are suddenly unavailable, leaving a coworker to explain how ill you became. When you realize how noncooperative that associate is being, you say nothing to her but vow to get even by "accidentally" forgetting to tell her about next week's meeting with key clients until five minutes before the meeting.

The following list describes some typical passive-aggressive behaviors. Do you recognize any of them?

- Saying you will do something, knowing you won't do it to that person's satisfaction.

- Talking about a person's negative traits behind his back, sabotaging his reputation.

- Procrastination.

- Refusing to make a commitment, even when a commitment is needed.

- Withdrawing in punitive silence.

- Deliberately avoiding someone when open discussion is needed.

- Pretending to be agreeable while you disdain what the person says.

The passive-aggressive approach ultimately subverts any relationship. As long as you are in such a mode, trust cannot be established. Significance cannot be sustained because relationships have a "gamy" or manipulative feel.

## PLAN HEALTHY ANGER

If you can agree it's possible to choose to manage your anger, then you have hope. While resolving conflicts and tension may not always be easy or pleasant, you can make great progress as you choose to act in a way consistent with personal significance.

Let's examine two options of anger management that can keep significance alive, both in yourself and others.

1) *Assertive communication.* When you hear the word *assertive*, what comes to mind? Pushy? Blunt? Forward? Abrasive? By "assertive" some people mean, "You just get out there and say whatever needs to be said, and if others don't like it, that's their tough luck." Such folks may use the word *assertive,* but *aggressive* is a more accurate term.

Assertive anger means you are willing to preserve personal worth, needs, and convictions, *while also* being considerate of the worth of those with whom you are in conflict. For instance, in our hypothetical problem, you might say to the insensitive boss, "I will do the best I can to get the report done by tomorrow, but I want you to be aware that it will take a day or two longer to complete it as thoroughly as you want." When he snaps back and says get it done anyway, you can hold your ground without apology: "I'm going to give it my best effort, but I'm also going to remain honest in what I say can and cannot be done by tomorrow." No harshness in your voice, just calm firmness. To the associate who has been uncooperative you might say, "I'm disappointed you didn't come through with the help you promised. I'm moving forward with my part, and if you can help me, here is how you could do so. If you choose not to help, let me know now so I can plan around it."

Speaking assertively does not guarantee that the receiver will like what you have to say, but making her like your words is not your goal. The goal is to be caringly honest and responsible.

Look over the following examples of assertiveness. How natural are they to you?

- You openly stand up for your convictions without succumbing to a combative spirit.

- You let your needs be clearly known.

- When pushed to follow unreasonable expectations, you do not let yourself become a doormat. Instead, you do what you are reasonably capable of doing.

- You ask for favors or help when appropriate.

- Rather than agreeing with something wrong, you do what is right.

- You set personal boundaries and stipulations in a calm, confident fashion.

- You know when to say "no" or "not now."

True assertiveness helps sustain your own sense of significance because it does not allow you to accept demeaning or nonaffirming behavior. Likewise, it maintains an attitude of significance building because it upholds others' dignity. You can be in disagreement without being disagreeable.

Wise individuals understand that conflict in relationships is inevitable. Not only do significance-building persons assert themselves, they openly welcome and encourage others to do so as well. But therein lies a catch. Not everyone wants to so assert themselves. Fed by a false pride that keeps them self-focused, they may attempt to squelch assertiveness. You may choose to hold onto your healthy assertions despite their resistance, or you may choose the next option.

2) *Releasing anger.* Circumstances will arise that make you angry, yet you may quickly conclude, "Though I have a legitimate reason to feel angry, I'd rather not give it any energy or attention. More important matters need my focus."

Go back once again to our hypothetical illustration. You may feel angry at the boss for saddling you with an unrealistic deadline, but you may inwardly conclude, "All I can do is my best. I'm going to make every effort to please him and do a good job. Once I've done that, if he's frustrated with me, so be it." When the associate fails to follow through, you may think, *I know she's not good at setting schedules and talking straight, so I shouldn't be surprised that she's promised more than she can deliver. Next time, I'll be more careful in what I ask of her.*

Look over the following responses and determine how you could implement any of them:

- You know the value of forgiveness, so you are willing to forgive when appropriate.

- You accept the reality that people can be imperfect, sometimes aggravatingly so.

- You are not easily shocked by rudeness or insensitivity. In fact, you make room for it.

- You are aware of your limits and know you cannot make life always comply with your wishes.

- You are committed to inner composure and are aware that it results from a choice.

- You realize you are not bound to join others in irresponsible behavior.

- Your mood is guided by an inner compass, not by external circumstances.

For most people, releasing anger is not easy or natural. Some even wrongly assume it requires that the emotion be suppressed. Releasing anger is *not* the same as suppressing it. You release anger as you realize you have higher goals to attain, goals like acceptance and kindness and a level temperament. Releasing anger does not imply weakness, but strength. It shows that you possess an inner fortitude not tied to external elements. Your emotions do not have to resemble a roller coaster ride, rising and falling according to every bend in the track.

By appropriately releasing anger you can value significance, both your own and the people in your world. You choose not to allow yourself to be bogged down in fruitless haggling, and you demonstrate to others that you can still treat them with respect, even when it has not been earned.

## The LIFT Model and Anger

While significance-building choices can lead the way in helping you to manage your own anger, another challenge also needs attention. How should you respond to someone else's anger, particularly when they use it wrongly?

Let's go back to our illustration of Steve, the software engineer who had to work with the self-centered Harry. Not only will Steve need to understand his own anger and make appropriate choices regarding its direction, he must have a good idea about how he will respond to Harry's anger.

On Steve's first day back to work after abruptly leaving the office, Harry was his usual abrasive self, barking orders and acting bossy and overbearing. "Hey Steve," he bellowed, "I've got to have your help on this project. Get me some numbers from the Aberdeen file. You're going to have to determine if we can put their proposal together within budget. Old man Jones is breathing down my neck and needs an answer yesterday."

Steve knew he would be unable to comply with this demand while also meeting his own tight deadlines, and it angered him that Harry assumed the world revolved around his needs, but rather than suppressing his anger like he normally did, Steve decided to assert himself. "Harry, that's not something I can do this morning," he replied. "I'm tied up with my own problems. You'll need to check the Aberdeen file for yourself."

Harry was unaccustomed to being told no. He was not Steve's boss so he couldn't pull rank, yet he tried to push his agenda in his typical bully fashion. But regardless of the coercion, Steve chose not to budge. This made Harry angry. Rather than being overwhelmed by Harry's anger, Steve could use the LIFT model of transactions. Here's how it could work:

*Listen.* As Harry angrily told Steve he'd better get to work on this project, Steve could ask himself, *What's driving Harry's anger? Why does he so frequently feel like he's got to have his way?* Steve could recognize that Harry's excessive anger was propelled by his fear of being deemed insignificant. Harry believed that if he developed a softer form of communication, no one would take him seriously. In spite of his loud and blustery ways, Harry was an insecure man.

*Identify.* Steve could identify his options for the moment. He could enter into a war of words with Harry . . . though it would probably produce an ugly fallout. He could succumb in fear. Or he could stand his ground while also empathizing with Harry's plight. This would be his best option, prompting him to say, "Harry, I'm simply not able to go along with your request this time. I know you've got a big deadline, but you're a resourceful person. If anyone can handle the problem it's you."

*Force the appropriate response.* Once Harry registers his predictable protest, Steve can stand his ground by saying, "You know, I frequently lay aside my projects to help you; nonetheless, this is one of those times I'm not going to be able to do that. I hope you'll understand." No further defending or explaining is necessary.

*Target significance-building transactions.* Harry is likely to be angry with Steve, spending the rest of the day in a foul mood.

Steve, however, could choose not to respond in kind. He could continue the rest of the day in calm confidence, speaking supportively to Harry when appropriate.

Being committed to significance building does not require you to cower to someone else's moodiness, nor do you have to abandon your resolve to be firm. Your commitment to significance will prompt you to stand for what you know is right and best, while continuing to act with the other person's dignity in mind.

## Let Anger Work for You

This chapter assumes that conflict happens. It is unavoidable, since any gathering of imperfect people with varying priorities will inevitably produce friction. Whether you are in sales, management, product development, marketing support, customer service, or instruction, you simply cannot expect continually smooth personal exchanges.

By exploring your options of anger management, both good and bad, you can anticipate what to do when conflicts arise. People show their true character not when relationships progress smoothly, but when conflict becomes acute. Are you willing to accept the challenge to be a significance builder, especially in those moments?

When you respond to conflict by properly asserting yourself or by releasing it in favor of greater priorities, you demonstrate a calm and confidence that people learn to trust . . . and you also communicate respect to those involved. As you respond to conflicts over the years and months, you establish a reputation that either enhances or diminishes your opportunities for career advancement.

Let your response to anger be known as fair and balanced. Learn to anticipate the likely circumstances that cause conflict and poise yourself for a significance-based response. When you witness others managing conflict wrongly, choose not to respond in kind, but instead determine to be a stabilizer. When you do, you will find you have conquered your own greatest adversary, yourself.

Once you learn to make good choices in handling anger, you will be ready to respond well to people who pose ongoing difficulty. In the next chapters, we will identify some of the more common difficult personalities and how to disconnect from their "hooks," thereby enabling you to reach your greater goals.

## UNDERSTANDING ANGER

- *Can you remember at least three ways that anger can be recognized in a person's behavior?*

- *Can you look at yourself and identify at least two ways that you express your anger?*

- *Are you able to identify the significance roots in some of the ways you express your anger toward others?*

- *It has been said that depression is anger turned inward. Do you agree with that statement? Can you explain why you agree or disagree?*

- *Review the steps of the LIFT model and verbalize how you would use it to deal with a person who is faced with the challenge of personal anger.*

- *Under what circumstances is anger healthy?*

- *Can you think of ways that anger can impact the effectiveness of someone at work or in a social setting?*

# Chapter *Seven*
## DEALING WITH DIFFICULT PEOPLE

The traveler presented his documents to the immigrations officer-in-training. Within moments a supervisor arrived on the scene, looked over the documents, then turned to the trainee and said, "Am I going to rip this guy, or what?" And rip she did, even threatening to send the traveler back home due to a minor error in his paperwork.

Why is it that some people get their kicks by ripping people? Difficult people are a major roadblock to your efforts at significance building, and dealing with them requires a deft ability to avoid the traps they lay.

Have you ever had trouble dealing with someone and later discovered the individual had relational difficulties with everyone? Some people apparently get up in the morning intent on having a bad day . . . and they are often just as committed to making sure *you* have a bad day. Your challenge is to stay the course despite their efforts to sabotage your sense of significance.

# Seven Difficult People

In order to help you deal with difficult people, we would like to introduce you to seven character types who represent a majority of the difficult people you encounter.

## 1. THE SABOTEUR

On the surface, saboteurs seem pleasant enough; they often give the appearance of being quite friendly. But therein lies the problem. They operate with a double agenda, appearing to be an ally while at the same time undermining the people and circumstances they do not like. A saboteur may tell you how well you have handled a project, then tell a coworker, "It's a shame he can't pull his load around here." Like a stealth fighter, saboteurs penetrate your defenses and do their damage before you know what's happened.

Saboteurs typically nurse high levels of anger, but are very cautious in exposing it. Somewhere along the way they concluded that direct or open confrontations were risky, so they began using indirect means of pushing their agendas. If you have ever dealt with a saboteur you know such a person can cause substantial damage in your sphere of influence before you ever realize the source of that damage.

Qualities common in the saboteur include:

- He likes getting the scoop regarding "inside issues."

- She often will say what a person seems to want to hear.

- He will fluctuate on his opinions, depending on the "atmosphere."

- Loyalty is given to the ones who are currently in power or in the know.

- She invites people to trust her.

- He tells you confidential information with the condition that you not repeat it.

- She somehow seems to be up-to-date on all the latest news.

- You are never quite sure if he is truly what he claims to be.

## 2. THE ROMAN CANDLE

The roman candle personality is like a fireworks display—an explosive eruption. Persons with this disposition often express strong displeasure with little provocation, leaving people wondering, *Where did that come from?* Observers see little or no reasoning for such outbursts, often causing them to conclude it is wisest to keep a safe distance . . . which is probably what the roman candle wants.

Like the saboteur, a roman candle also struggles with anger, though it is more blatantly displayed. These persons often express Rodney Dangerfield-like sentiments: "I don't get no respect." Usually they have two common problems fueling their anger. First, they have come to believe that people will not listen to them unless they are emphatic. Second, they live with a fear of not being thought of as significant. What is worse, many will not take responsibility for the damage they inflict, often saying things like, "Look what you made me do!" In their mind, they are rarely at fault.

Common traits of roman candles include:

- A strong sense of correctness.

- An ongoing feeling that others just can't be trusted to do things right.

- Difficulty saying, "I was wrong."

- People skills do not come naturally.

- Believes intimidation is a good way to motivate others.

- Operates with tunnel vision.

- Surprised that others are so offended by their anger.

- Power is their ultimate thrill.

## 3. THE HELPLESS CONTROLLER

Young children learn quickly that if they whine, someone will pay immediate attention. Most of us excuse this behavior in youngsters, but when adults carry this to the extreme, it can feel very manipulative.

People with long-standing insecurities often believe they may not be deemed significant if they discuss their needs in an open, objective manner. This can cause them to develop a strategy of helplessness whereby they play upon the sympathies or the good nature of others to get what they want. They can be described as high-maintenance takers who use their apparent helplessness to elicit constant reassurance of their significance. These people are virtually impossible to satisfy, since they always want more. While helpless controllers tend to sit on a lot of anger, the depth of such an emotion can be difficult to recognize early in the relationship because they are skilled in covering offensive personality traits.

Among their common tendencies:

- A charming style of relating.

- Frequent smiles accompanying flattering statements.

- Indecisiveness.

- Comments of appreciation that actually reflect great need.

- A "what have you done for me lately" attitude.

- Open self-doubt.

- Moving on once a relationship has been sucked dry.

## 4. THE GENERAL'S ASSISTANT

GAs attach themselves to people of power. While it can be wise to follow the guidance of a trusted mentor, that is not what GAs do. Realizing they may not be able to attain power on their own, they vicariously take on the power of the person to whom they are linked. For example, an administrative assistant may speak to others as if the chief were speaking, or a mid-level manager who just had a meeting with the CEO may begin statements with, "According to Mr. Bigsby, you're supposed to . . ." GAs want to achieve their own personal objectives, but they realize they have to use the higher-up's name to do so.

While GAs may appear confident, even arrogant, inwardly they are hiding a low view of themselves. By borrowing the strength of someone else, in essence they imply, "I'm not confident enough to feel significant based on my own merits." What is more, they often find it "helpful" to their egos to look upon others with disdain.

Common traits of the general's assistant might include:

- Blind loyalty, even if it seems illogical.

- An "us vs. you" manner of thinking.

- Being very turf conscious.

- Feelings of jealousy or possessiveness toward the general.

- A frequent tattletale.

- An "I don't need you" approach to people not in the loop.

- A major need to appear important.

## 5. PINOCCHIO

The Pinocchio personality has a problem telling the truth. In many cases these people set their sights on positions of influence, then achieve it. But over the long haul they may have to jump from one position to another to stay ahead of their lies. Although unlike Pinocchio their nose doesn't grow when they tell their lies, these people often develop reputations that are hard to live down.

While this personality may not struggle with anger, he does have serious problems with relationships in general. Many Pinocchios suffer from the chronic feeling of being runners-up in the contests of life, so they rationalize that it is okay to spice up their reports and achievements in order to find equal footing with the true big shots. Often their need to delude others is a direct by-product of their own self-delusions. They cut corners and tell half-truths so often that they no longer recognize that such a pattern is wrong.

Common traits of the Pinocchio personality:

- Making good first impressions.

- Making grand promises he cannot fulfill.

- Keeping secrets.

- Exaggerating personal achievements.

- Strong need to be approved.

- History of many positions and endeavors.

- Assumes that people should be impressed with her.

- Shifting opinions, depending on who he is talking to.

## 6. THE HYPER-CONTROLLER

Hyper-controllers need to be on top of everything. They are fearful, distrusting people who assume that others should not be given choices or could not have separate perspectives, because that could undermine the hyper-controller's precious power base. Consequently, not only are these types very opinionated about how projects should unfold, they also want to control the opinions of others. They tend to attract individuals who are weak and pliable, because these folks will not threaten their egos.

Hyper-controllers are often perfectionists who demand that everything should fit in its exact place. Driven by a strongly critical spirit, they believe most people cannot be counted on to do things right. As a result, they often think they have to do everything themselves.

They may have a wide range of acquaintances (particularly if so required by their work), but on the personal front they are loners who keep to themselves, revealing very little about who they are. Though they would never admit it, they are terribly insecure people who dread being "found out."

Common traits of hyper-controllers include:

- Inability to find what is good in others.

- Deep distrust of others.

- A cautious, calculated approach to life.

- Frustration when others share different perspectives.

- Ability to simply cut relationships off when they are no longer suitable.

- Stubborn, even when it leads to self-defeat.

- Not team players.

- Insensitive to the hurt they cause others.

## 7. THE BOOMERANG

As a kid did you ever play with a boomerang, throwing it out and watching it return to you? In the same way a boomerang returns to the one who throws it, boomerang personalities always find a way to turn a conversation back to their favorite subject: themselves.

When told that someone else won an award, the boomerang might reply, "That reminds me of the time I won the top employee award," then launch into an interminable story about himself. These people are definitely "takers" in that they believe they must take the focus off of others and put it on themselves, where it belongs. All the while they are oblivious to how they rob others of significance.

Common traits of the boomerang include:

- An inability to empathize with others.

- A history of broken relationships.

- Extroversion, but an accompanying shallowness.

- Easily upset when the spotlight shines on someone else.

- Requires constant attention and affirmation.

- Expects special favors and can become angry when they are not given.

## Developing Strategies for Dealing with Difficult People

One problem in dealing with difficult people is that you just don't think the way they do. Therefore you feel awkward when

*Challenges are inevitable;*
*defeat is optional.*

challenged or put "on the spot" by one of these people. Many times they design their approach to keep you off balance.

Before we examine some of the tools that can help you to disconnect from these difficult people, remember two words: *awareness* and *choices.*

*Awareness.* Some people are simply not committed to solid people skills. While you no doubt have a strong desire to live with balance and fairness, you cannot assume that everyone in your world shares similar priorities. While you cannot change the fact that some people are chronically difficult, by recognizing their problems you can keep yourself from being blindsided and falling victim to their negative tendencies.

*Choices.* While it may seem odd that some people actually choose to act in the ways just described, it is a fact that all behavior is the result of choices. You can determine to choose to live in significance-building ways. Though difficult people may "invite" you to respond to their poor choices with your own poor choices, you can determine to keep acting in ways consistent with significance. Stand on your own strength and resolve that you can resist nonproductive patterns of relating.

With that in mind, the following describes some tools to keep you from falling into the clutches of difficult people.

## Disconnection Tools

Have you ever felt as if you just couldn't escape from one of the personalities just described? Have you ever felt overwhelmed by them? If you want to continue living with a sense of significance, it is important to "disconnect" from unhealthy patterns, preferably before you get too deeply involved with them. Disconnecting allows you to keep necessary boundaries and gives you the opportunity to reconfirm that you will take appropriate directions in your life. There are five techniques or tools of disconnection.

*1. Restatement.* When people are forced to hear their own words repeated back to them, they often find they must rethink what they said. Take a typical example: "I want to hit Janet every time she talks about our problems in customer service." "Oh," you respond, "you want to hit Janet?" "Not really . . . you know what I mean." Notice that simply by restating the exact words spoken, you are able to do two things: First, you buy time to think about what you want to say; second, you are able to move the conversation to a more fact-based discussion—your original goal.

*2. Reflecting.* Reflecting is different from restating in that the goal is to take what was said and reword each topic so that it reflects the deeper meaning. Reflecting statements often begin with phrases like, "Oh, what you're really saying is . . ." or "I get the idea, what you mean by that is . . ."

Be aware of the pitfalls that may accompany reflecting. If you are not deliberate in your choice of words, the reflected statement can sound sarcastic. In other situations, the reflecting statement can be so clear that the sender may be offended by the reality of their own words. Consider the following transaction between a subordinate and a supervisor.

Subordinate: "At ABC Company, people like Debra would have been dealt with in a very decisive manner."

Supervisor: (Reflecting) "It sounds as if you are suggesting that she be terminated."

Notice that while it may have been the sender's intention to get Debra fired, he was unwilling to accept the responsibility for suggesting it. By reflecting upon the implied meaning of the statement, you encourage open honesty . . . something the other person may fear.

*3. Crystallizing.* The objective of crystallizing is to offer a broad summary of the communication. A difficult person often uses many words in an attempt to disguise what he means. As you carefully listen to the verbiage, you can succinctly synthesize them into one simple idea that crystallizes everything a person has said. The idea is to summarize the communication in order to disconnect with its irresponsible aspects and to affirm your intention to honestly respond with facts.

*4. Interrogating.* Difficult people often communicate high levels of anger or insecurity. To remain focused on your healthy course, you must refrain from being pulled into an emotionally charged exchange. The interrogation approach—asking questions—can be a very effective way to do that.

Suppose, for instance, you are accused with an offense so preposterous that you are caught speechless. Or imagine that someone (like the roman candle) explodes at you, putting you off balance. In such situations interrogation may have great value. For example, you may ask, "What are you trying to tell me?" or "What is your suggestion meant to imply?" Sometimes the simple asking of a question can get the conversation pointed toward a nonmanipulative dialogue. Through interrogation you affirm your commitment to adult-to-adult conversation.

*5. Recognizing (normally used with 1–4 above).* Before you use one of the four disconnect tools, it is often effective to use "recognition" to begin your conversation. It can often be as simple as, "Boy, it looks as if something has really made you upset. Would you like to tell me about it?"

This type of approach often stops people in their tracks. Imagine an irate customer storming up to a customer service person, expressing his anger in full force. The respondent might calmly reply, "It looks like we have done something to make you feel upset. Let's see what we can do to correct the problem."

In taking this action the customer service person is applying the significance principle. By recognizing that a person is upset, he is basically saying, "You are important and should not have been treated this way."

A number of years ago a man went to a major bank to apply for a car loan. He had been through some difficult times, but his business was starting to turn around and he thought the bank would consider all the facts in looking at his loan. He really needed a new car.

The banker was quite friendly until he looked at the man's credit report. When the banker realized the man had some credit problems, he demeaned the man in every way possible. The man left, dejected and embarrassed.

A number of years later, the man returned to the same bank, opened a new account, and transferred over a million dollars into the account from another bank. When the bank president saw the deposit on his daily report, he excitedly called the man and asked if they could have lunch. The man agreed and asked the president to bring along one of his loan officers (the one who years before had turned down his car loan).

For this lunch the president insisted on eating at one of the nicer restaurants in town. During the meal the president began thanking the man for his new account and asked him how he had decided to move such a large amount of money to his bank.

The man responded by telling the story about the loan officer who had embarrassed him so completely. He concluded by saying the one million dollars was being moved to another bank even as they ate, much to the displeasure of the bank president. "This was the only way I knew to make a point," the man said. "I wanted a way to explain to you guys just how awful it is to treat someone the way you treated me when I was a little down on my luck. Maybe the next time you will be nicer to people who come in and ask for a loan."

Difficult people—in this case, the loan officer—cost businesses time and money. Chances are, the president of the bank had a pretty good idea of how his officer handled people like this, but as we often all do, he chose to ignore it rather than deal with it. In this case, he learned a million-dollar lesson. He just learned it a little late.

We all have to deal with difficult people, whether they be coworkers, friends, or subordinates. Your challenge is to sustain significance-based thinking as you deal with such people. The chart on the following page shows how this can be accomplished.

As you accept the challenge to respond appropriately to others even as they make contrary choices, you will need to be armed with right thoughts and attitudes. There is one major trap you will need to avoid as you interact with difficult people: the temptation to control. Each of the difficult personalities profiled in this chapter has the desire to control. If you respond to their control behavior with your own control behavior, you will only get pulled down to their level. Let's look instead at a coaching approach that can allow you to effectively address problems with difficult people without getting drawn into control battles.

## An Effective Coaching Model: The Paraclete Approach

People in all walks of life often find that they are required to deal with someone who needs to change direction. In some cases, it may be a subordinate. In others, it may be a peer. Regardless, the principles of effective coaching are the same. We have found several ingredients that might be helpful in developing an effective personal coaching model.

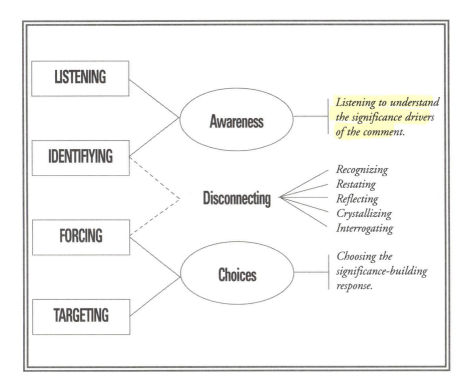

The Greek word *paraclete* was used by soldiers over two thousand years ago. It is actually a combination of two words, one has the idea of "coming along side" and the other has the idea of "exhorting" or calling out to someone. We believe the essence of the word portrays the basic behavior of a significance-building leader: one who comes alongside to encourage. However, leaders often have to deal with performance problems. You will discover that this coaching model works quite well with difficult people.

A significance-building model for coaching would follow a well-thought-out process, which targeted "win-win" for all parties. The following is the approach we recommend:

1. Establish the reason for visiting with the individual. Be up front with your motives for asking for the meeting. Avoid any appearance of control. (Asking for a meeting,

then not giving the reason, can be a form of controlling behavior.)

2. State your understanding of the problem. Be clear, not sly, about what you know about the individual's problem. Avoid hidden agendas.

3. Openly solicit that person's perspective of the issue. Make it clear that the discussion is an open exchange, not a lecture.

4. Express problems in the context of positive aspects of the person's performance and character. You might say: "I know you try to maintain very high work standards . . ." Or, to the Roman candle, you might say: "You became a little excited during the sales meeting. That tells me you have a passion for what you do . . ."

5. Establish clear goals and standards of acceptable performance. Without engaging in imperative communication, make it clear that you still have certain bottom-line goals and standards of performance. Focus on your desire for them to be successful.

6. Affirm that all actions are a result of choice. Acknowledge that significance-destroying behavior is a choice, just as significance-building behavior is a choice. Voice your comments so that the individual understands that his or her future will be a result of choices made. It is his or her option to choose.

7. Get agreement and commitment. As you reveal, by your behavior, that you are interested in their success as well as the organization's, help them understand which choices will meet both goals.

8. Follow up your meeting with accountability and encouragement.

Keep in mind that this coaching approach will be successful only if you already have a reputation for being a significance builder. Your ability to coach difficult people will establish that you expect each person within the organization to be responsible for his or her own behavior. By the way, there are a few common mistakes you should avoid when confronting difficult people:

- Assuming that the other person's perspective is inferior or inadequate.

- Immediately peppering them with solutions instead of using leading questions and appropriate agreement to let them develop their own solutions.

- Asking condescending questions (such as: "Since you always seem to drop the ball in this area, how do you plan on correcting this problem?").

You will find that it is during these potentially stressful moments that your reputation will be established. Look at conflict or problems as an opportunity to make a positive difference in the lives of others.

## DEALING WITH DIFFICULT PEOPLE

- *Identify some "difficult people" you have to deal with.*

- *Try to classify each one of these people according to the seven types listed in this chapter.*

- *Recall some specific situations where the ability to deal effectively with difficult people could have changed the outcome.*

- *Which of the "disconnection" tools best fit your personality?*

- *How might you best deal with the difficult people in your life?*

# Chapter Eight
# COMMUNICATION: IMPERATIVES AND EMPOWERMENT

Everyone has standards of right and wrong. The standard may vary from person to person, but we each have notions about what should be.

And it is precisely those notions that can inhibit the building of significance.

"But we *must* have some moral codes to guide living," you respond. "How could a person's beliefs about right and wrong be harmful?"

While we would never oppose a system of moral absolutes—that is the first step toward chaos—we do believe it is possible to have too much of a good thing.

Imagine you receive an invitation to a friend's house for a large dinner party. You are especially honored to be a guest, since this event is attended by popular and influential people. As you approach the front door, your friend greets you with, "Before you enter, we need to go over a quick item of business." He then produces a neatly typed document, which reads, "House Rules: Here is how you must act in my home." Twenty-five items are spelled out, including: "You must be patient"; "You must be respectful"; "Don't criticize, but be an encourager"; "You cannot use foul language"; and so on.

After reading aloud all twenty-five items, the host hands the document to you and says, "Sign here on this line and come on in." How are you going to respond?

If you are like most people, you will feel very uncomfortable, even insulted. But let's suppose you decide to comply. You sign the document, enter the man's home, greet people you know, get a drink and some finger foods, and try to settle in with some friendly conversation. About fifteen minutes later you feel a tap on the shoulder. You turn around and encounter your host, who is smiling and holding up your signed document. "Excuse me, but we have a small problem," he says. "You'll notice on item number eight that you are supposed to be friendly. I've been watching you, and while you've done fairly well, I'd like you to pick up the pace."

That said, your host leaves and you return to socializing, determined to do your best. In another fifteen minutes you once again feel a tap on the shoulder. "Pardon me for interrupting again," says the host, "but let's do a quick review. Would you reread item seventeen and tell me in your own words how it would apply to your behavior with these people?" After the review you are released and you determine to live correctly, according to the document's specifications.

Now imagine that this same correction occurs several times more throughout the evening. By the end of the dinner (assuming you last that long), what emotions would you be feeling?

First, you'd be angry (or at least quite frustrated and irritated and annoyed). You would also become cautious and calculated, thinking *I've got to figure out how to get this pesky person off my back.* Depending on your makeup, you may even develop some guilt and insecurity, wondering, *What is so wrong about me that*

*I keep missing the mark?* Your emotions would be anything but pleasant.

Now shift gears and focus on the host. What emotions would he be feeling as the evening progressed? He wouldn't be much more composed than you! He, too, would feel irritable and annoyed, though for different reasons. He might be harboring some self-doubt and worry: *What is it about me that causes my guest to disregard my rules?* Impatience and tension would also likely plague him.

As absurd as the illustration may seem, it parallels the experience of many people who have felt robbed of their significance. It is quite likely you have encountered people who push their agenda regarding right and wrong. These people feel so strongly about their convictions that they try to make sure you act according to their code. They probably don't carry around a formal document, but they don't have to—they are more than ready to remind you of what you should do.

A man once summarized this problem by explaining, "I'm so right, I'm wrong." He had so many notions of correctness that he felt justified in being critical or bossy or impatient or stubborn or noncooperative. His right notions became the impetus for disastrous relationship habits.

## The Negative Results of Imperative Thinking

People whose notions of correctness are so strong that they adversely affect their relationships suffer from what we call "imperative thinking." Imperative thinking can be defined as a control manner of thought that ultimately neglects the significance needs of others. The easiest way to spot it is to listen for key words: *have to, must, can't, should, supposed to, got to, need to, had better.*

About 99 percent of the time, such a strong element of truth accompanies this imperative thinking that the communicator feels justified in its use, oblivious to the negative effect it may have on others. An imperative thinker may correctly tell a coworker, "You've got to write your reports in a different fashion," yet unknowingly also be conveying, "I think you're a dumb bunny." Or perhaps he may rightly say, "We have to treat our suppliers with respect," unaware that he may also be suggesting, "I'm not sure I can count on you."

Imperative thinking takes proper behavior to an extreme while also sabotaging the necessary relationship skills that ensure teamwork and cohesion. Spoken words may be accompanied by an army of silent messages that run contrary to the oral communication.

Every communication contains two forms of messages, overt and covert. The overt message is the spoken word, while the covert message is the implied meaning. In successful communication, the covert messages far outweigh the overt in importance, yet we typically give more thought to the overt messages than to the covert. Are you aware of these two levels of communication? To successfully build significance, value and respect must flavor both forms of messages.

Let's return to Mr. Vickers, the executive of the small business that we introduced in chapter 4. Though he seemed to do everything right on the surface (giving employee-of-the-month awards, sending memos extolling the value of each employee, etc.), his company suffered from low morale. Why? As the consultant discovered, his spoken words did not accurately reflect his deeper attitudes. While he may have said, "You're really valuable to me," he was so particular about how business had to be conducted that his employees felt devalued. And while he would enthusiastically declare at staff meetings, "We're all necessary

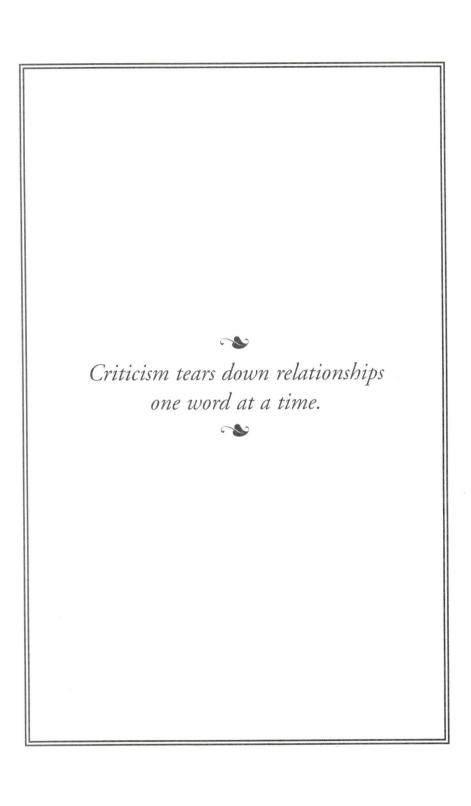

*Criticism tears down relationships*
*one word at a time.*

ingredients of the team," he became extremely defensive when someone made suggestions that did not coincide with his preferences.

Mr. Vickers could speak all day long about the necessity of his people, but as long as he nursed an imperative thinking pattern (with its many musts and shoulds and have to's), he was stifling the creativity of his people. And ultimately he inhibited any sense of loyalty toward him.

People want to feel necessary, and when they do not, they either go somewhere else or they become disgruntled.

If imperative communication appears so right on the surface, why does it ultimately fail? Because it overlooks an overwhelmingly powerful ingredient in human nature: the yearning to be free. Imperative thinking is anchored in the illusion that people can and will be controlled. It ignores the reality that each person possesses a free will that compels them to choose their own destiny. The successful management of people requires that the bedrock quality of freedom be fully acknowledged.

When we talk about freedom in our consulting sessions, we usually get one of two responses:

1. "Hey, freedom! I like that. Sounds like a wonderful idea to me."
2. "Wait a minute. Freedom? Sounds like a formula for irresponsibility and disarray."

Certainly freedom can be abused, but that is part of the risk of letting people be who they are. And what is the alternative? Controlling people ultimately does not work.

People eventually resist being controlled because their need for self-determination compels them to find the means to remain true to their real self. When denied the privilege of choices, people will simply become more creative in finding ways to express their individuality.

Let's consider these thoughts in light of two major truths:

1. Control (the goal of imperative thinking) is an illusion.
2. Freedom is reality.

Structure and accountability and common goals are necessary to a successful organization, yet organizations also need to make room for choice. Yes, there is risk in allowing choices; but good leaders will encourage choices within reasonable boundaries, and in doing so will create an atmosphere ripe for loyalty and cooperation.

If indeed control is an illusion and freedom is reality, then why not openly live within reality? Why be a dictator when cooperation can be fostered through the allowance of choices? Why tell people how they must behave when they would appreciate the opportunity to express their uniqueness? Why keep minds confined to one fixed agenda when many options can better take you to your goals?

## Five Factors of Empowerment

Two parents were discussing their philosophies of child-rearing. One explained forcefully, "As a parent, it is my job to tell my kids what is right and wrong and to make sure they do right even if they don't like it." The other parent replied, "I'm all for teaching my kids right and wrong, but I have something else in mind when I talk to my kids. I'm aware that I won't be there forever to tell them what to do, so I try to teach my kids to take ownership of their beliefs. I try to put as many choices as possible in front of them, helping them to understand the consequences of each choice, then freeing them to select their best options."

Which type of parent would you like to have? One focuses exclusively on outer results, while the other focuses on building the inner person. The second style requires more self-restraint, but it is likely to yield far greater rewards.

Think about these two differing approaches in adult relationships. Which would you prefer, the tell-you-what-to-do approach, or the examine-the-options approach? Most adults do not want to be treated like children who are denied the privilege of choice. (For that matter, most children don't like to be denied choices, either.) Assuming themselves to be competent, reasonable persons, they want to know they can exercise options.

Empowerment is the path to organizational teamwork. Bottom-line results can still be achieved. Accountability can be in place. Yet individuals can feel permitted to be just that, individuals. Personal uniqueness can be allowed even as team unity is sought.

It is simple enough to suggest that empowerment should be part of any adult interaction, but the lust for control can be intoxicating. Letting go of control and openly empowering others requires that you lay down some ego and take a chance on others' capabilities. Are you up to it?

Let's examine five qualities necessary for creating an atmosphere of empowerment.

## 1. PERSONAL ACCOUNTABILITY VS. MICROMANAGEMENT

Whether an organization has four people or forty thousand, a delicate tension exists between relational criteria for success and a financial bottom line that must be satisfied. To meet those goals each individual in the organization will go about his or her business with a unique combination of strengths, weaknesses, ideas, quirks, priorities, emotions, and perceptions. Not one of them can be made into something they are not. Every person is unique.

The tension arises when efforts are made to impose "group-think" on such a collection of individuals. Individuals can be ordered to leave their personal uniqueness at the door and to fit their habits into tightly regimented slots, but this never works for long. In such an atmosphere of micromanagement, fine details of a person's work habits are scrutinized, even if it sacrifices the effectiveness of the group. Short-term compliance is valued over long-term competence.

Sound too absurd to be real? Consider the remarks of people who have been there:

- "My manager doesn't know anything about the personalities of the people I encounter every day in the field, yet he constantly insists that I present my products only in the formats approved by him . . . and he's very picky in what he requires. I wish he could spend a week out here using his own stupid techniques so he could see how ridiculous his requirements are."

- "I finally found a way to communicate some hard concepts to my students. They're really catching on and we've got some major creativity flowing in the classroom. I'm having to fight off the principal because her favorite phrase is: 'But we've never done it like this before.'"

- "There are so many forms I have to fill out for my projects that it takes double the time to get anything done. What's frustrating is that the forms add absolutely nothing to our finished product. They just satisfy some higher-up bureaucrat's need to feel necessary."

Sound familiar? Have you ever felt so stuck in the mire of micromanagement that your contributions to overall goals are less than what they could be? More importantly, do you concentrate so strongly on the methods involved in problem solving that you inhibit others from attacking problems creatively?

Group goals and personal significance can be pursued simultaneously; one does not have to cancel out the other. Accountability can be put into place in the form of quotas or deadlines or measurable criteria that can satisfy the larger group's need for proven progress, and once these things are established, individual uniqueness can be allowed. Never assume that there is only one way to do a job well.

## 2. PEOPLE-FOCUSED VS. PERFORMANCE-FOCUSED

Some people erroneously assume that if you champion personal issues over performances, you must want to turn every meeting into a group therapy session. That's not true. What we're suggesting is that in getting to a successful bottom line it is incredibly easy to forget that people, not merely performers, get you there.

Consider these comments from employees at a middle-sized business:

- "It was a delight to have Janice lead our team. She could stay focused on the task, yet she made me feel like I truly mattered."

- "Janice remembered the name of my son's baseball team. That may seem insignificant, but it let me know she cares about me as a person."

- "Just before I left the office, Janice stuck her head in my door and told me she hoped my weekend at the in-law's would go well. My last boss couldn't have cared less."

- "Before our budget meeting, Janice called me to get some extra details on a unique proposal I'd mentioned to her. She told me I had a knack for coming up with out-of-the-box ideas that challenged the group. I really like her."

Who is Janice, and what makes her so special? She is the office manager at a company that handles lab records for medical doctors. Her employees were under constant pressure to keep the doctors satisfied, and their last manager pressed so hard to keep the doctors happy that his tense manner produced the opposite effect.

When Janice took over, she set the pace by explaining, "I'm assuming you each are qualified to do what you do. It's not my job to do your work for you, but to be a sounding board if pressures get in the way of doing your work. I need to hear from you if we're going to be most effective."

*"I need to hear from you."* Those were foreign words to the technicians, who were used to being ignored (meaning they hadn't fouled up). The atmosphere at the office long ago lost its personal flair because personal expressions were quickly squelched. Janice changed that by saying, "We're all here to do a job, so let's do it well. But in the meantime, let's remember that life consists of more than just processing medical records. It's important to keep a sense of balance."

Unlike Janice, imperative people prefer to disregard all things personal since personal issues cannot always be categorized into neat packages. Janice kept her focus on company priorities but got a greater effort from her people because she never became so busy that she could not take a moment to add a personal touch to their transactions.

### 3. DESCRIPTION VS. JUDGMENT

Imperative communicators typically earn a reputation as judgmental. Imagine a stuffy teacher with glasses at the end of her nose, staring and pointing at you with a bony finger. Or picture a gruff taskmaster with harsh opinions about everything and everyone, opinions he's anxious to loudly express.

The people in your world may not be like a stuffy teacher or gruff taskmaster, but you may be painfully familiar with the atmosphere caused by someone with a judgmental spirit. You know it's curtains if someone makes one false move or misses a specification.

Consider how common the mind of judgment is and recognize its effect on personal significance. From your earliest days you have been rated and graded and judged. At school your work was graded and your self-esteem adjusted accordingly. With peers certain behaviors were deemed acceptable or not. At home you knew the rules and were judged as good or bad based on your compliance. As an adult your performance has been scrutinized and you have been judged based on compliance with others' norms.

How can judgment or evaluations inhibit personal significance? They imply that you are only as good as your latest achievement. Even when you receive an excellent judgment, there is a threat: "You'd better continue doing well, or you'll be told you are not adequate." By their judgmental nature, imperative people tend to create a "one up, one down" feeling in their relationships. By so doing they create disincentives for teamwork while encouraging bland conformity. And productivity suffers.

So what is the alternative?

Descriptive communication allows you to be honest about your beliefs or priorities without also being judgmental. This manner of thought seeks to explain perceptions and needs while also refusing to condescend. Here are some examples:

- Instead of saying: "You messed up again, this work isn't cutting it," describe what you observe and what you need. For instance: "Your thoughts were on a different wavelength than mine. I think your mind is fascinated by some of the details that go beyond the scope of the project. Let's refocus."

- Instead of saying: "You did a good job handling that difficult phone call," show that you truly comprehend what happened. You could say, "When that caller lost his cool, I guess you toyed with the idea of giving him some of his own medicine, but you chose to take the high road instead. I've noticed how you have a knack for adding calm to a potentially tense situation."

What's the difference between judgment and description? One puts life on a scorecard, the other sees beyond the performance into the person. One implies an ongoing threat to keep up the grade, while the other makes room for the human factor. One causes people to wonder where they currently stand on the totem pole, the other communicates acceptance of differences.

Significance builders still have criteria to measure success, but they are willing to take the time to think creatively as they speak to others. Rather than focusing only on how well a person did, they notice the behind-the-scenes processes that went into the effort. Not content to speak only to the outside of a person, they notice what is inside and how it relates to performance.

## 4. PRINCIPLE-DRIVEN VS. DUTY-DRIVEN

A young boy being punished was told to sit in his chair until further notice. "I may be sitting down on the outside," he muttered defiantly, "but I'm standing up on the inside."

Imperative communication forces conformity, yet without true inner agreement. Imperative people are satisfied when the external looks fine, but they do not realize how forced compliance undermines long-term loyalty. For instance, a computer design researcher once explained, "I did everything asked of me by my higher-ups, but I didn't like it one bit. Not once did they ask me how my duties fit with my own beliefs or ideas. I realized I was a robot being trained to do but not to think."

For people to feel significant and to claim ownership of a dream, they need to believe their own principles and beliefs are an integral part of their efforts. They want to sense that mandate somehow fits with their life's mission. For instance, an insurance claims worker was required to take information from people obviously frustrated with unexpected problems. Her wise supervisor said, "It's one thing to fill out the forms correctly and process the information efficiently, but I wonder if you can see how your effort fits into the larger picture?"

Pleasantly surprised that her supervisor would address a behind-the-scenes issue, she replied, "I guess it's part of our service to let frustrated people know that someone is on their side, trying to ease the aggravation associated with their claim." The two talked openly for several minutes about the good their company provided and about the need for each of them to act upon their deeper understanding of their service.

Principles, not sheer duty, make a person feel like a contributing part of an organization. While imperative thinkers worry only about the bottom line, significance builders focus on developing the rationale in people that causes them to feel necessary and to pursue excellence. The "I have to do it" mentality gets traded in for a mentality that says, "I know who I am and where I'm going."

## 5. ENCOURAGEMENT VS. CRITICISM

If imperative communication produces anything, it is an atmosphere of criticism. The imaginary dinner host at the beginning of this chapter hardly exuded friendliness. If anything, he would be known as a critic who can't be satisfied.

When your communication is heavily flavored with "have to" and "should" and "got to," you will quickly develop a reputation as one who cannot be pleased. Your covert messages declare, "I don't accept you in your current state" or "I'm not sure you can be trusted" or "You're inferior to my standards." People who are constantly told what to do or who receive hard directives with no leeway are likely to feel insulted. Likewise, when people get excessive, unsolicited advice (something imperative people do constantly), they feel they are not cutting the muster.

As an alternative, consider how people can be motivated with words of encouragement. In your organization, workplace, church, or home, how often are words of edification spoken? Do others free you to find your worth by telling you things like:

- "You really make a difference around here."

- "I'm amazed at your ability to organize things so quickly."

- "Your spirit helps generate enthusiasm with the team."

- "I truly look forward to hearing your take on matters."

- "I noticed that extra effort you made—way to go!"

Likewise are you one to frequently give away such words?

Every organization must pursue its bottom line, yet the best path to that bottom line is significantly rewarding when liberally accompanied by encouraging words.

# A Real-World Example

Before giving a talk to a group of senior managers of an international firm, we were approached by the vice president responsible for the division. "Just do me one favor," he said. "Explain to these people why every plan we've made for the day is blown away by a crisis by 10:30 A.M. If you can do that, we will at least leave here understanding why we are all so frustrated in our jobs." While we confessed we couldn't alter the competitive environment, we did have some ideas that could help.

Much of our work is for firms competing in chaotic environments. To survive, such organizations must learn to eat change for breakfast. How can you best deal with chaotic environments? Before we give you our take on the problem, we would like to tell you about Mr. Johnstone, the new vice president of the leading competitor of the firm just mentioned above.

Mr. Johnstone knew how to get things done. He knew how to shape up an organization. So when he was promoted to his new job, he decided to get the place in shipshape. He walked in with more than ideas on his first day on the job; he walked in with a stopwatch.

At exactly 8:00 A.M., he positioned himself by the front door. He had one of his new employees accompany him with a clipboard to record Mr. Johnstone's comments. As each person entered, he would ask the assistant for the name of the person entering. The comments went like this:

"Washington: 30 seconds late."

"Smith: 40 seconds late."

"Bianconi: 2 minutes 31 seconds late."

"Sergi: 4 minutes 45 seconds late."

This went on until every employee arrived at the office. Johnstone finished the exercise, convinced he had made his point and confident every employee now knew who was boss and what was expected.

What Johnstone missed was that his new organization was serving customers in a highly chaotic and competitive environment. Competitors threw new products at this group faster than they could respond. The team already was working sixty to eighty hours per week. Johnstone failed to realize that instead of control and imperative communication, his employees needed empowerment and encouragement. He was too focused on his own picky agenda to notice the real needs of his people.

Remember the three keys to Southwest Airlines' success?

1. Encourage others as a way of life.
2. Have fun (don't take yourself too seriously).
3. Commit to excellence.

Johnstone missed on each one. His imperative approach was guaranteed to kill the spirit, the aggressiveness, and the creativity of his new team. And he didn't last long. His imperative approach was so destructive that he was relieved of his job a short time after he arrived.

The point is simple: Imperative communication robs others of the joy of their work, their accomplishments, and their associations. Imperative communication is a veiled attempt to build ourselves up at the expense of others. More than that, imperative communication, if allowed to become a way of life in an organization, robs it of its performance and ultimately might kill it.

In the next chapter, we will take our thinking a step further by discussing the necessity of tuning in to each employee's perspective.

## IMPERATIVE VS. EMPOWERING

- *How often do you find yourself using words like should and must?*

- *As you look back over the last year or so, describe anyone you can identify as an "imperative person."*

- *Have you ever worked for a truly empowering manager? How did he or she make you feel about yourself?*

- *In your experience, what percentage of people tend to be imperative communicators?*

- *What possible benefits can be derived from imperative communication?*

- *What changes in communications could your organization make to enable it to become more like Southwest Airlines?*

# Chapter Nine
# LEADERSHIP AT ALL LEVELS OF THE ORGANIZATION

It's frustrating when you need to get something accomplished but you keep running into puzzling internal roadblocks. It's equally frustrating to try motivating someone to do the right thing, only to find that he will not do it and is unwilling to tell you why.

Why does defensive posturing so often become part of an organization's communication style? Because the leadership has not created an environment where people feel safe. Often in these cases, the issue of power lies at the heart of the problem. And power, when fully understood, is clearly a significance issue.

Solid leadership is necessary to keep internal turf wars from mushrooming. An organization that fails to curb jealous jockeying for position will likely be ineffective or chaotic—and often will implode.

Regardless of where you stand on an organizational ladder, you can wield some influence as you humbly uphold human significance. When people become impatient or insecure or disillusioned, however, they often abandon good practices in a hungry grab for power. This effort to find power causes them to concentrate on how to retain power—and left far behind is the common good of all.

Consider, for instance, the many cases in which companies have announced their intention to computerize their operations, only to encounter serious resistance. Rather than focusing upon the benefits to both the public and the company, many employees focus upon what they perceive as "potential problems" with the new system. They are so intent on protecting their own significance that they shift into a stubborn power mode. The net result is what we call *power paralysis*.

> POWER PARALYSIS: WHEN THE POSSIBLE LOSS OF POWER OVERRIDES THE ABILITY TO DISCOVER AND MOVE TOWARD THAT WHICH IS BEST FOR THE ENTIRE ORGANIZATION.

Power paralysis can occur at any level of an organization. Leaders at each level must know how to manage organizational needs while remaining aware of individuals' significance needs. The people at the top can set the pace as they illustrate good leadership, but they need to openly encourage others beneath them to follow their example. Some CEOs and executives may be threatened by this possibility because their imbalanced significance needs prompt them to assume that only they can lead. But secure executives want many leaders to shine. In fact, the more, the better!

Leadership requirements differ as you move up or down the bureaucratic ladder, but leaders at each position must be freed to exercise their influence in ways that improve the entire organization. In the pages to follow, we will examine how leadership can flow from the top, the middle, and the bottom of organizations.

# Leading from the Top

Leaders at or near the top of an organization face a unique set of challenges. Those at the top are expected to display an extra level of expertise; they should not struggle with "what to do" questions in the same way subordinates do. Instead, they're supposed to be the "go to" people. Sometimes this pressure comes from outside sources, while at other times the greatest enemy is within themselves.

Consider, for instance, the pressure facing university professors. As professors, they're supposed to be at the top of the heap. They're expected to know the latest trends and developments in their field and are supposed to be able to clearly communicate the many aspects of their subject. Students, of course, are supposed to revere them for their knowledge. Yet as one professor put it, "After they graduate, they don't have the same feeling toward you. It's as if they've figured out that you really are just human."

Isn't it the same way with top-level management? They really are just regular folks, but they're supposed to know more than they actually do and are not supposed to need the input they actually require. It is crucial for these people not to allow the pressure of false expectations to dictate their manner of dealing with people. Business consultant M. Scott Myers stated several years ago that we often ask the wrong people to solve organizational problems. His conclusion: The people doing the job, not the CEO, know more about solving the problem related to their job. What a novel thought!

Successful top-level leaders not only accept their limits, they openly acknowledge their need for input. For instance, let's suppose a firm's salespeople have information critical to the company's success, but are dismissed because, after all, they're just salespeople. This happens too often in many organizations (the unsuccessful ones). Good CEOs want input from all levels.

Some may ask, "But doesn't this diminish the CEOs sense of significance when he or she has to acknowledge limits?" Not if you keep in mind the significance paradox. By keeping an open door to a broad array of subordinates, that CEO is reinforcing their significance. This in turn creates a sense of team, increasing subordinates' respect for the one at the top. Saying the words "I need help" does not have to denote incompetence. Instead it can instead signal that you highly value those in your organization.

When you value people equally, your organization will perform at a high level. Why? The reason is simple. Forty thousand people can know more than two; eighty thousand ears can listen better than four; forty thousand brains can process more information than two. When you convince people that you truly consider them significant, they will share with you their person—that is, their knowledge, their ears, their brains. When your actions convince them you deem them as necessary and valuable, they become willing to participate in your success.

Ironic, isn't it? If you try to keep the credit for yourself, you will enjoy little success. If you give credit to those who make possible your organization's success, you will receive far more credit, even though that is not what you seek.

So how to do this? Start by answering a few questions about your leadership style.

- Do your subordinates view you as an obstacle or an encourager?

- Do you encourage an explorer mentality among your subordinates?

- Do people suggest they have to manage around you to do the right thing?

- Do you like hearing different ideas?

- Would your subordinates say that you truly listen and take action on their input?

- Do your subordinates view you as a resource person?

To get the most accurate answer to these questions, you might try venturing out into the workplace and asking your subordinates to answer them for you. You might be surprised (shocked?) to hear what they might say. Often companies hire corporate psychologists to come in and test these issues. Would you be willing to listen to their findings and receive the honest input of those who work under you?

## FIVE CHARACTERISTICS OF EXECUTIVE LEADERS

Serving at the highest levels of an organization is both an honor and a tremendous responsibility. To be most effective, your own significance needs must be addressed even as you seek to build others. Those who consistently succeed at this level tend to exhibit the following qualities:

*1. They are good listeners.* Perhaps you have heard the old saying, "You have two ears and one mouth; listen twice as much as you speak." Listening is not the same as hearing; listeners not only hear the spoken words, they ponder them. Good listeners encourage people to bring information to them, even if they ultimately disagree with that information.

Strong leaders have confidence in their own abilities, yet they are wise enough to know they have blind spots. They realize that each personality is predisposed to receive and interpret information differently. Some focus on one aspect of a problem, others focus on another. Rather than summarily dismissing others' perceptions, they hunger for outside input. They know someone else may have interpreted events in a way they completely missed.

Several years ago an insurance claims filer at a medical office approached the owner of the medical clinic. "My job seems to be changing every week," she said. "Our patients are coming in with health plans that are radically different from the insurance coverage we're used to." The doctor's first inclination was to dismiss the clerk by saying, "We've done fine with the insurance companies up to this point; let's not worry about a few things here and there that don't match our procedures." Instead he asked, "What are you suggesting?" She devised a way of searching out the new health plans and actively seeking their referrals, and thus recognized the new wave of managed health care then in its infancy. She and a coworker hustled to learn as much as possible about thriving in the new system. Months later when similar medical clinics were either downsizing or merging with other facilities, this medical clinic was thriving and expanding.

Top-level leaders realize they cannot be expected to be experts at all elements in their field. Information is too extensive and volatile. Change is too inconsistent and erratic. Not only do they willingly listen to their people, they unleash them to be additional "ears" and information gatherers whose input is treated like a prized possession.

*2. They are never stuck on the status quo.* Too many leaders assume that the best way to manage problems is to repeat what was done in the past. While a keen sense of history can bring perspective on where you are today, it is dangerous to build strictly upon the past.

Regardless of the nature of your organization, there is far too much volatility to rest on historical strengths only. The successful leaders of today live in a mode of anticipation regarding tomorrow. They virtually never say, "This is the way we've always done it." Instead, they remain open to innovations and actively encourage others to challenge the status quo.

*3. They are not impressed with power trappings.* We know an executive of an energy consulting firm who makes a seven-figure annual income. He refuses to buy a car less than two years old. "Being financially wise is what my business is all about," he says. "Why, then, in my personal life would I manage my money in a way inconsistent with my business philosophy? I'll let the auto value depreciate on someone else's watch, then I'll buy a still perfectly good car for a much greater value."

This man is more than financially prudent; he is unimpressed by the look of power. He could have anything he wants, yet he knows that power and prestige can become props for an insecure person who feels the need to be set above his constituents. Like a good leader, he wants to remain close to his people. He has determined that if the superficial appearance of power creates gaps in relationships, he will forego it. But how could his employees possibly know about his personal practices? "Whether they know about my personal practices or not, I know," he said, "and I don't ever want to feel too impressed with myself."

*4. They are transparent.* You can see through transparent substances. Glass, for instance, is transparent; you can peer directly through it and view what is on the other side.

Now apply this idea to personalities. Transparent leaders have no hidden agendas. They are direct and open and don't leave you guessing about their motives. They also feel no need to feed their egos by putting up a false front.

Leaders can be tempted to use their role to manipulate others, to coerce or trick others to satisfy their own preferences (even when it may be less than good for all involved). Significance-building leaders want nothing to do with this pattern of relating. They would prefer the motto, "What you see is what you get." Their yes means yes and their no means no.

Transparency ultimately leads to trust, since subordinates do not constantly have to decipher hidden meanings. It also creates a feeling of respect in the subordinates, since they know they are being managed with no hidden agendas.

*5. They can maintain confidentiality.* People at the top of an organization gain a broader knowledge of many facets of that organization. New arrivals to the penthouse often express amazement at the many tidbits of information they were not privy to when in a lesser capacity.

Leaders at the top, more than anyone else, need a broad grasp of information to make good decisions. Therefore they tend to learn of behind-the-scenes problems or not-for-public-consumption information. These leaders show themselves to be trustworthy when they choose not to gossip, when they keep confidential matters confidential, and when they refuse to use privileged information for personal gain.

## Leading from the Middle

Have you ever watched a "tug of war" contest? Two groups of people, one on either side of a large mud puddle, start pulling until one side wins . . . and the other side gets wet and filthy. Welcome to managing in the middle of an organization.

People who find themselves in the middle soon discover that it may be one of the most unenviable of places. It is usually the people in the middle who have to relay unpleasant news from the top of the organization to those at the bottom. They also have to listen to those below them and convince them that the higher-ups really do care about their opinions and problems. In many ways, middle managers are the most frustrated people in the organization. They feel stuck in the messenger position—and as everyone knows, it is usually the messenger who gets shot. They hear about problems from both the top and the bottom, yet typically lack the power to effect changes.

Have you ever known anyone who just couldn't handle the middle of an organization, with pressures from both above and below? Have you ever known someone who got there and did really well? Most of us have known both kinds of people. Those who do well might be identified as people who lead well right where they are.

What does it take to lead from the middle? The following five characteristics suggest the necessary qualities. As we examine these qualities, keep in mind that successful mid-level leaders are able to lead, not because of the position they are in, but because of the qualities they possess.

## FIVE CHARACTERISTICS OF PEOPLE WHO LEAD WELL FROM THE MIDDLE

*1. They are eager learners.* Okay, so it is awkward to hear of problems from people both above and below you. Yet think on the bright side. Most ideas and perceptions meet in the middle of an organization. In the middle there is much to learn and tremendous insight to be gained. Mid-level managers, in their role as bridge builders, will succeed as they sustain a keen curiosity about what makes people think and react as they do.

Mid-level managers are likely to hear from the CEO about the direction of the company and the need to keep a sense of vision, as well as from the "ants" who are likely to describe procedures and operations problems. Which groups of ideas or thoughts are most valid? They both are, and the good mid-level manager knows it. Rather than declaring themselves for one side and against the other, they assume there is too much to learn to be argumentative.

Instead, they like to listen patiently and are unwilling to jump to quick judgments.

*2. They are decisive.* Their role in the middle of an organization does not require these leaders to become wishy-washy. Mid-level leaders can show what they believe and champion causes. Rather than worrying about being liked (which indicates questions about their own significance), they concern themselves with being fair and right. They are willing to act, not just react.

Good mid-level leaders realize that because of their in-between status they will not always succeed, yet they feel a sense of honor when they stand and say they did their best.

*3. They are people of integrity.* One of the most common temptations in the middle is to play both sides off the other. For instance, if higher-ups complain about lagging productivity, middle managers might reply, "Boy, we've got to kick some tail in the ranks." Then when subordinates gripe about not being highly regarded, the MMs might chime in, "Someone's got to show those egomaniacs they can't get away with this abuse!" An overeagerness to be liked by all can cause middle managers to live with watered-down convictions.

Mid-level leaders committed to significance do not allow themselves to get caught in such a Ping-Pong match. They seek to be known as fair-minded toward both the higher and lower ends of the spectrum. While they may feel short-term discomfort as others attempt to improperly persuade them, in the long-term they usually enjoy a solid reputation. Others realize they cannot be swayed by short-sighted conversations. Mid-level leaders know that integrity ultimately benefits everyone in the organization, and as their reputation is established, they are used increasingly in decisive roles.

*4. They are risk-willing.* A commitment to integrity and decisiveness implies that mid-level leaders are risk takers. What's so risky about decisiveness and integrity? Seasoned veterans know that "political correctness" is often rewarded over honesty; those who are willing to hedge the truth or to cut corners to keep others happy may find some level of reward. It is not always popular to be straight-laced.

Successful leaders, though, look out for the good of the whole. Playing it safe for the sole purpose of self-protection harms an organization. Strong leaders are willing to explore new frontiers. They want to know why and they thrive on new and unique ideas.

*5. They are aware of their limits.* Insecure people have trouble admitting their influence is minimal. Delusions of grandeur cause them to wonder why other people do not always heed their advice or follow their suggestions. When these people allow themselves to assume their influence should know no limit, they set themselves up for great frustration and severely inhibit their ability to lead.

Strong leaders are confident and believe others should hear what they have to say. Yet they are also pragmatic. They realize that not everything will proceed as they wish. Rather than pushing their agendas on every issue, they carefully select what they will fight for. For instance, one mid-level manager, Stan, was pulled aside by a wiser team member, who told him, "You've got great ideas that the group needs to hear, but you comment so frequently on so many issues that your message is being diluted. You can't win every battle. When you recognize you have limits, your reputation will improve. Right now your excessive opinions cause people to view you as just another critic."

Stan realized his friend was correct. By acknowledging his limits he was able to increase, not decrease, his status within the organization.

If you lead from the middle of an organization, ask yourself the following questions:

- Do people feel comfortable in bringing me unpleasant or bad news?

- Are people willing to share information with me that could harm them if I violated their confidence?

- If I allowed those who report to me to give an anonymous assessment of my strengths, would they say I am willing to take their ideas to the top?

- Do people believe I will take risks to do the right thing?

- Do people view me as a politically oriented person or a people-oriented person?

## Leading from the Bottom of the Organization

During a major battle, a lieutenant in Napoleon's army realized that the tide was turning against his side. As he watched one soldier after another turn and run in fear toward the back lines, he asked himself what he could do. Suddenly it hit him. He began laughing and pointing at the soldiers who were running from the battle. A few noticed what he was doing, then more, and finally a number concluded that what they were doing must be really stupid since he was laughing at them.

It didn't take long for those who had run toward the back to hear that the battle had taken a turn for the better. As they returned, the enthusiasm of the troops mushroomed and the entire line began moving forward . . . to victory.

One lowly soldier really can turn the tide of battle, as this true story illustrates. In the formal structure of things, the people at the bottom are usually perceived as those who do what they are told. In reality, it is the people at the bottom of an organization who take charge of their own future and in turn positively affect the future of many others. More often than not, it is the people at the bottom who change the organization.

It makes sense, doesn't it? After all, it is the people in contact with the customer, those who do the basic jobs, who often know the most about what the organization really needs. So what makes people effective leaders at the bottom of an organization? The following five traits usually pop to the surface:

### FIVE CHARACTERISTICS OF PEOPLE WHO LEAD FROM THE BOTTOM

*1. They are scarce.* People who lead well from the bottom have a reputation for hard work. They have little time for office politics or schmoozing up to the boss. Rather than trying to get by with glib words or empty self-promotion, they prefer to set an example with their disciplined work. They are willing to do the necessary behind-the-scenes jobs that keep the organization flowing smoothly. They realize that, in time, they gain credibility because people respect them for their integrity. Others know they are not inclined to waste time, theirs or that of others.

*2. They are tenacious.* Leaders at the bottom of an organization know they don't have a glamorous position, yet they press on because they realize their significance does not depend upon outer signs of prestige. They are aware they may have to deal with rejection; they understand that some higher-ups may have trouble giving credit to them for better ideas.

These leaders realize that hard work is its own reward, and they know that ultimately it will be difficult for others to ignore them. They earn a reputation as tenacious and believe in the tenet "Actions speak louder than words."

*3. They are supportive.* Strong top-level leaders value diversity and realize that innovation is born out of many ideas. Yet even as they seek diversity, these people want to know that those beneath them display loyalty. Bottom-level leaders realize this and do not begrudge the fact.

Though they are not always privy to top management's thoughts, bottom-level leaders usually have good notions about where the organization is headed and they want to be a part of its success. To that end, they show enthusiasm for their work and so let higher leadership know they can be counted on. They like their role because they realize that when they do a job well, everyone gains.

*4. They look for creative opportunities.* "Dreariness" needn't be a synonym for serving near the bottom of an organization. Creative ideas do not flow only from the top. In fact, the "hands-on" people are most prominently positioned to suggest helpful adjustments.

Leaders at the bottom are not content to go through the motions of work, but want to help the greater unit. This enthusiasm for quality work and exemplary skills prompts them to search for new ways to approach tasks.

*5. They have a feeling of equality.* Those at the bottom of an organizational ladder can easily assume they hold an inferior status. Leaders at this level do not allow themselves to think such a thing. While they acknowledge legitimate authority and varying levels of skill and ability, they do not interpret "different" to mean "superior."

The human body has many parts that service the whole. It would be odd to have more than two ears, or to say to the kneecaps, "You're unnecessary," or to belittle the pinkie finger for being small. Each part of the body has a separate function and each is necessary in its own place. So it is with organizations. The leader of a "lesser" unit knows that while it may not be the "central nervous system" or the "heart" of his organization, it serves a necessary function.

Leading from the bottom often involves personal risk. We don't always have time to "call home" to get permission to solve a customer problem. Consider the story about a Xerox salesman who ran into an interesting problem.

# The Xerox Solution

On a routine trip to a major customer in Arkansas, a salesman discovered a Japanese-made copier sitting next to one of Xerox's copiers. The company had hundreds of Xerox copiers at this site and he was concerned about the presence of one of his competitors' machines.

When he asked about the machine, he was told that the company had been having problems with the Xerox policy on copier repairs. At that time Xerox set repair priorities based upon the size of the machine. Large copiers received quick service, but small copiers often sat broken for one or two days. The salesman then was told that the Japanese company promised if it got the account, *all* of the copiers—not just the large machines—would be repaired within three hours of going out of service. Was that the only problem the customer had with Xerox, the salesman asked? Yes, came the response.

Although it was a Friday afternoon, the salesman decided he needed to take immediate action. The customer's account was so large that an entire team had been assigned to it, but the salesman reached every Xerox representative, one by one, and got them to agree to meet immediately.

The team met through the entire weekend. By Monday they had developed an aggressive service program for the client, one that guaranteed that every copier, no matter what size, would be repaired within three hours. The team set up twenty-four-hour, on-call schedules for the entire team and developed a notification system, which gave the client confidence that Xerox would always be able to deliver. The team met with the client and offered its

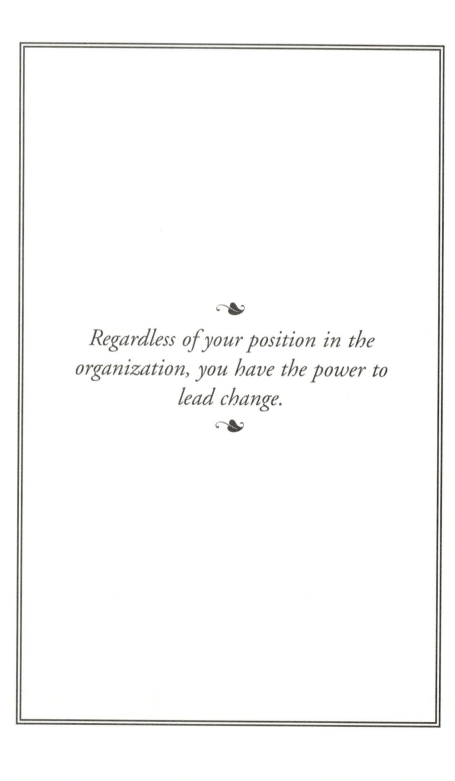

*Regardless of your position in the organization, you have the power to lead change.*

proposal, which was received with enthusiasm. Xerox kept the account and the next day the competitor's copier was removed.

But there is more.

The team was so focused upon solving the problem that it had no time to advise superiors of the problem or of the commitments about to be made. Once they reached agreement with the customer, the team went to management and *advised them of what they had already done.* And their solution was accepted with enthusiasm!

How many people do you know who would be willing to put their jobs on the line to solve a customer problem? How many executives do you know who would be willing to let their subordinates commit the company to an agreement with long-term implications for the firm?

The real key for becoming a high performance organization is to create an environment that fosters change. That means changing the organization so that everyone is a leader . . . at all levels.

## LEADERSHIP

- *Compare your position in your organization with the five characteristics of people who lead well from that level. Score yourself on how you think you would do.*

- *How would you fare if those who worked with you answered the same questions about you? If you have an internal consultant in your organization, are you willing to ask for a poll to find out just how well you lead?*

- *Write a list of the benefits to your organization that you believe would occur if it had "leadership at all levels."*

- *What must you do to bring about the benefits you named in the previous question?*

# *Chapter* Ten
# MINING THE INTELLECTUAL CAPITAL OF AN ORGANIZATION

> EVERYTHING THAT CAN BE INVENTED HAS BEEN
> INVENTED.
> Charles H. Duell, U.S. Commissioner of Patents, 1899

Jonathan understood the astonishing challenges his organization was facing. In fact, he had understood them for years. As a subsidiary of a major international firm, his company had long enjoyed a reputation as a leader in the field of corporate training. But that period of success was nearly over.

Remembering the preceding five years, Jonathan noted the times he had tried to convince his superiors that technology was about to bring earth-shattering changes to their field. He knew that as the technology changed, the training tools also would change. Not only that, but the rapid emergence of the Internet as a training medium would radically change price structures in their industry.

Jonathan's superiors gave lip service to his concerns, but continued to turn their backs on his ideas. And now it had happened. Every warning he had given had blossomed into a present threat. But this time it hit the firm where it hurt the most: its largest customer.

By using a lot of the ideas Jonathan had been advocating, the firm's largest competitor had just gone to its best customer and hit a home run. When told that their largest competitor had pulled off the coup, one senior manager responded, "I thought we owned their business."

But this was more than a coup. In a single stroke, the competitor figured out how to raid Jonathan's firm and *land revenue that exceeded the total of all the remaining clients in Jonathan's firm*—and all this from a customer that Jonathan's superiors thought they owned!

How could such a thing happen? How could an entire executive team ignore the obvious? Doesn't their job description include keeping the company abreast of such mammoth changes?

Perhaps, but the sad truth is that such events happen every day. Why? Because most people do not understand the concept of "mining intellectual capital." And even if they do understand it, they have no idea how to do it.

> WE DON'T LIKE THEIR SOUND. GROUPS OF GUITARS ARE
> ON THE WAY OUT.
> Decca Records' rejection of the Beatles in 1962

## Intellectual Capital

What is intellectual capital? Is it what the "new products" group of a firm develops? Hardly. Intellectual capital is not the exclusive domain of a research team nor is it the special treasure of a think tank. Intellectual capital is potential income. It is potential products. It is the collective creativity and market intelligence of an entire organization.

# The NIH Syndrome

At the very root of mistakes regarding intellectual capital is the notion that good ideas come only from the top. This phenomenon has come to be known as the "not invented here syndrome" (or NIH Syndrome). The problem exists when those at the top of an organization feel compelled to reject any idea not their own, regardless of how important the information might be. This concept is fraught with significance issues.

Jonathan, the individual in our opening story, went to his superior about the changes he saw coming to the industry. While his superior listened politely, he responded, "I have formed a committee to study this issue. I am sure we will be at the leading edge of all such issues." (Translation: "Jonathan, you are not significant because you are not a corporate officer like I am. Therefore, Jonathan, your input cannot be important, because you are not an important person.")

People who are color-blind cannot distinguish certain colors, no matter how hard they try. What if you discovered you were color-blind, and yet were assigned a job that required you to search for and report on the very colors you couldn't see? What would you do? Would it make sense to find partners who could see those colors and ask them to team with you on the project?

> THERE IS NO REASON FOR ANY INDIVIDUAL TO HAVE A
> COMPUTER IN THEIR HOME.
> Kenneth Olsen, President of Digital Computer, 1977

Intellectual capital is just like that. According to extensive research by Everett M. Rogers,[1] the intellectual capital of an organization is rarely found in the senior executive team. In fact, the personalities represented on the senior executive team usually have the most trouble in recognizing the value of the intellectual capital that can save the firm. Michael Tushman[2] confirmed in his research that during periods of extreme change, it is often necessary to replace senior executives if the organization is to deal with the surprises of a changing environment.

This suggests that as the world changes, those who have the power to deal with the change often refuse to listen to those who can solve the problem. They refuse to listen to those who possess the intellectual capital to move the firm to the next wave of profit opportunities.

The quotes in frames in this chapter ran in a 1997 edition of *Newsweek* magazine. The source article pointed out all the opportunities that had been missed because people just did not see change coming.[3] Organizations of all types are increasingly talking about change and what they can do about it. Change affects us as individuals also. It is quite common for us to resist change, only later to find out how badly our resistance hurt us. That's where intellectual capital comes in. It allows us to see change and to realistically deal with it.

Each of us works from a "personality of change" that describes how we change and why we resist it. Every organization has some high-level "learning personalities," but often we do not listen to them. Here are a few questions to consider as we talk about change in organizations:

- Do you find something wrong with every new idea that someone suggests?

- Have you ever discouraged someone on an idea, only to discover later that you were wrong?

- Have you ever been absolutely clear about an organizational problem, but no one would listen to you?

- Do you know anyone who seems to be willing to listen to the ideas of others?

- Have you ever seen someone strongly resist a new idea or a change, even though it was a good idea and could help the organization?

The survival of an organization often revolves around its ability to understand and effectively deal with change. Organizations that do this well are often called "learning organizations." Organizations that learn well are able to maximize the importance and significance of their people because they understand their potential. They understand the concept of intellectual capital, the awesome potential of their people who can convert their knowledge into profit opportunities for the firm.

All of us have blind spots when it comes to change. It is almost impossible to get past those blind spots—unless you learn how to effectively team with others whose own blind spots do not overlap yours. So how do you deal with your blind spots and effectively compensate for them? It all begins with understanding the "Five Personalities of Change."

## The Five Personalities of Change

The work by E. M. Rogers[4] cited earlier noted how change occurs similarly across different societies and social structures. Rogers concluded that a number of studies taken together gave a clear picture about how change penetrates a social structure. It appears there are five personalities of change.[5] Once you understand the five personalities, it will become clear why it is so difficult to get the knowledge contained in an organization—the intellectual capital, if you will—to those who have the institutional power to effect change.

Rogers pointed out that learning is passed through five types of people, each one with a different predisposition toward change. In each organization, as well as in society in general, learning passes through each of these personalities in sequence:

1. The Pathfinder:      2.5%   of the population
                                      (the first to learn)
2. The Listener:        13.5%  of the population
3. The Organizer:       34.0%  of the population
4. The Follower:        34.0%  of the population
5. The Patriot:         16.0%  of the population
                                      (the last to learn)

Again, the learning occurs in order, starting with the pathfinder. (Much about the following characteristics is drawn from Everett M. Roger's work, a compilation of more than 1,500 studies done on this topic.)

## PATHFINDER (2.5 PERCENT)

Pathfinders are the first to see the future. They are the only personality which is not "paradigm blind." In our experience pathfinders are rarely senior executives of firms. The pathfinder is often a frustrated individual because he or she can see the facts

---

### Keys to Recognizing Pathfinders

OUT-OF-THE-BOX THINKERS

CONSUMED WITH THE FUTURE; SEE THINGS OTHERS DON'T

SOMETIMES GET CHASTISED BECAUSE THEY ARE TOO INTERESTED IN CHANGE

OFTEN SEE SOLUTIONS TO PROBLEMS, BUT FIND IT HARD TO SELL THEIR IDEAS

DREAMERS, VISIONARIES

---

*When we fail to value all of our*
*people, regardless of position,*
*we often lose by allowing much*
*of our intellectual capital*
*to walk out the door.*

so clearly while those around tend to reject the information. They often describe themselves as people who have to fight their management just to get them to do the right thing.

## LISTENER (13.5 PERCENT)

Listeners are the only people who give any credibility to the pathfinders. The listener personality is usually a respected member of the team, even though it is unusual to find them at the CEO level. It is not, however, unusual to find them in senior executive staff positions. Listeners are respected because by listening to others, they affirm the significance of those communicating with them. As a result, it is not unusual for executives to want to surround themselves with the listener personality. These people are often referred to as "champions" because they sponsor change in the firm. The key to this ability is their history. They have usually managed to gain significant power and respect because of their willingness to listen.

---

### Keys to Recognizing Listeners

NOT QUICK TO JUMP TO KNEE-JERK CONCLUSIONS

OFTEN SEEN AS A "RESIDENT EXPERT" IN THE FIRM

CAN TRULY ABSORB WHAT OTHERS ARE TRYING TO CONVEY

SOMETIMES ARE CALLED "CHAMPIONS" OF NEW IDEAS

STEADY AND RELIABLE

---

## ORGANIZER (34 PERCENT)

The organizer personality is where CEOs come from. They drive organizations to their highest potential. They are also resistant to change by nature. This is where the extreme irony of organizational learning occurs: The organizer has the formal power to encourage organizational change, but they tend to resist such change.

Something else happens as learning enters the organizer population. Rogers points out that once learning has passed through 25 percent of the organization, it is practically impossible to defeat the change (this suggests that once change has been driven through a mere 9 percent of the organizer personalities, it should be past the point of defeat).

---

### Keys to Recognizing Organizers

PREFER THINGS TO BE ORDERLY, SPELLED OUT

MODERATELY RESISTANT TO CHANGE

DRIVEN PERSONALITIES; FAST-TRACK MANAGEMENT TYPES

OFTEN EXTREMELY DETAIL ORIENTED

WANT THINGS IN THE CORRECT SLOT

---

## FOLLOWER (34 PERCENT)

Followers are extremely resistant to change. In addition, they usually detest the pathfinders because they have no use for the information the pathfinder tries to bring into the organization. Nonetheless, followers are valuable people to an organization. They are tenacious and can be a steadying influence on fellow employees. They are great sales types because they are capable of handling a lot of rejection. They are committed to the organization and greatly value their coworkers.

## PATRIOT (16 PERCENT)

We also refer to patriots as "diehards" because they are the last to consider change. As charter members of the "Flat Earth

---

### Keys to Recognizing Followers

CAN BE ENTHUSIASTIC OR LOYAL

VERY RESISTANT TO CHANGE

TENACIOUS, COMMITTED, ORGANIZATIONAL TYPES

OFTEN FOUND IN MARKETING/SALES JOBS; HANDLE REJEC-
TION WELL

VERY HAPPY WHEN LIFE IS IN PERSPECTIVE

---

Society," they have little use for the pathfinder personality and are often willing to start rumors about the pathfinders just to get them out of their hair. Patriots are the most change-resistant of all the personalities.

On the other hand, the patriot is the most organizationally committed of all of the personalities. They never give up.

---

### Keys to Recognizing Patriots

HATE THE PATHFINDERS; HATE CHANGE; WILL DO ANY-
THING TO AVOID CHANGE

THE MOST ORGANIZATIONALLY COMMITTED MEMBER OF A
TEAM

NEVER GIVE UP; MAKE GREAT SALES MANAGERS

CAN BE CRITICALLY MINDED

WILL AVOID CONTROVERSY, BUT MAY QUIETLY SABOTAGE
FREE THINKER

---

## The Links of Learning and Intellectual Capital

Now that you have been introduced to each personality, try this quick exercise. Think of a number of people with whom you have been associated in the recent past. Can you categorize each one according to personality type? Do you understand the importance of each personality? Do you realize it takes all of them for an organization to succeed?

We recently received a call from a high-tech research lab in Canada. They had taken our personality assessment and looked at how their linkage of personalities had affected two key research projects. One had failed miserably; the other was a smashing success. "Guess what?" the caller said. "This personality stuff *works.*"

"Really?" we responded. "Explain why you are saying that."

The caller then explained that on the failed project it was clear they had put follower and patriot personalities into the process much too early. On the successful project they had done just the opposite by linking pathfinders, listeners, and organizers to the organizer personality who headed the project.

## Significance and Mining Intellectual Capital

After a recent seminar, one participant came up and showed us a personality assessment he had completed on himself. It is rare to find a "flat-line organizer," a person whose every tendency indicates he or she is an organizer. We generally find that people usually show strong tendencies in two areas. In this case, the individual was 70 percent follower and 30 percent organizer.

We first commented that he would probably be excellent in the sales and marketing area. Then we suggested he was a very competitive person and could handle rejection easily. "Right on," he replied, adding that he was a regional sales director and was a top performer in his firm. Finally we recommended that he develop strong links with people on his team with high organizer tendencies; further, we thought he needed to develop strong links with a couple of pathfinder personalities to help him learn.

He had discovered he wasn't the best manager on his team, but had found a classic organizer who could keep his team on track all of the time. Additionally, he found that his boss was a strong pathfinder (60% probably) and organizer (40%), and they had developed an excellent ability to team up.

It quickly became clear this man had already done everything we were suggesting, and had done it quite well. Yet as we visited with him, it became apparent that despite his driven, competitive nature, he was also a transparent, humble man. Because he was willing and able to put his ego aside, he could put each person on his team, including his superior, in the right place. That way, they all won. In effect, he recognized the significance of each person so as a team they could achieve excellence.

Organizations that apply these principles on a broad scale tend to readily accept learning from everyone, from customer, to vendor, to employees. Such firms are able to focus upon the importance of all so they all can succeed. Interstate Battery System of America is one such organization.

## Interstate Battery System of America, Inc.

When John Searcy got into the battery distribution business in the 1950s, he probably had no idea how large his then-infant company would become. Early in the development of his local Dallas firm, John decided that he wanted to foster what he called "going the extra mile." To John, there was no difference between family, employees, or customers. He believed this had to be his foundational business principle.

John's business thrived under his leadership, and today Interstate produces almost half a billion dollars in revenue each year. It is now an international firm with more than 330 distributorships.

"Even though John is not active in the firm today, we still spend most of our time focusing upon the principles that John Searcy developed when he started this company," says Norm Miller, chairman of Interstate since 1978. "When we go out and work with our distributors, one of the most important issues we spend our time on is teaching them how to go the extra mile. Putting others first has been the key to building this business and that's where we really try to get our distributors to spend their time."

Norm Miller's enthusiasm for Searcy's business approach has not dwindled over the years. "When you do business with people this way—by treating them the way you'd like to be treated—people figure that out real quick," Miller states. "And when people figure out that your goal in life is to put them at the top of your list, they really want to do business with you."

Norm Miller is excited about how these principles have worked for Interstate and cites three results: (1) low customer turnover, (2) low employee turnover, and (3) ongoing momentum.

"People don't realize how much employee turnover can negatively impact your business," Miller says.

As the Interstate story reveals, companies that value their team as significant constantly undergo positive change and growth. It is that ability to value and mine your intellectual capital that creates organizations that exceed expectations.

One reason Interstate Battery enjoyed so much success in its early years was John Searcy's ability to create an environment in which his people felt they were valued. Because he invited pathfinders, listeners, organizers, followers, and patriots all to participate in Interstate's success, the firm prospered. And Norm Miller, by following Searcy's example, has taken the firm to new and exciting levels of excellence.

And there's no reason you can't do the same.

## MINING INTELLECTUAL CAPITAL

- *Recall instances where you were tempted to withhold critical information because of the way you had been treated.*

- *Have you ever recognized a problem before it occurred, only to have the people around you ignore your warnings?*

- *Have you ever watched a company get into trouble because they would not listen to their people?*

- *Based on this chapter, think of ways to create an effective employee suggestion program.*

- *How important to the growth of an organization is significance-based empowerment?*

# Chapter Eleven

# SELLING IS A SIGNIFICANCE TRANSACTION

*Oh no,* the salesman thought as he saw the Birminghams approach. He knew he should expect the unexpected, but was nonetheless courteous and greeted the couple with a smile and a handshake. Mrs. Birmingham started right off: "We have a few more questions about the car we're interested in, if you aren't tied up with a customer."

"Glad to help. What do you want to know?"

It was the sixth or seventh time the Birminghams had come in to look at the car, but you'd never know it by watching the salesman. He focused on their every need, even though by this time he must have been getting tired of the questions. The couple's new list of questions sounded an awful lot like their previous questions, yet the salesman responded to each one like a "friendly encyclopedia."

Mr. Birmingham had been trained in sales himself and noticed that the car salesman never tried to close the sale. The questions were asked and answered, yet the young man never asked for the couple's business. Finally Mrs. Birmingham looked at her husband and said, "I'm ready to buy; what about you?"

To the trained salesperson, failing to ask for the customer's business is the equivalent of buying a double chocolate brownie and never tasting it. But to this salesman, one of the best in his field, selling was more than closing just one sale. He understood selling as a relationship that needed to focus on the customer as a person, not merely as a transaction that ended when the sale was rung up.

## Selling Is More than Technique, System, or Method

All too often, people who get into sales think there is some magical method or approach they can copy to ensure success. New salespeople often make joint calls with successful salespeople and try to imitate what they see. The truly successful salesperson, however, understands that successful selling begins, not with wonderful techniques, but with being the person you are. Consider Joe's story.

Joe was an engineer, with a personality befitting a typical engineer. When Joe returned to get his MBA, some people were surprised because they could not envision Joe as a manager. He just was not very people- oriented. Upon finishing his MBA, Joe resigned from his engineering job and went to work as a commissioned life insurance salesman.

Once again, most people who knew Joe couldn't believe it, since he was the most deadpan personality they had ever met. Hardly anyone could imagine Joe ever making a sale; he seemed closer to a 1 than a 10 on a personality scale. Joe, however, viewed himself differently. He knew he was efficient, organized, and focused. He also realized he would never be a "slap on the back" salesman and he wasn't going to change his personal style.

Today, Joe is a millionaire. He manages his own portfolio, which he continues to build out of commissions from life insurance sales. His six-figure income allows him to continue building that portfolio, and he is facing imminent retirement with ease. If you were one of Joe's clients, his success would be no mystery to you. Joe is able to use his preoccupation with organization and detail to make himself into one of the most client-focused salespersons imaginable.

Even now, Joe's manner is no different than it was twenty years ago when he entered the business. His deadpan voice, clipped and colorless speech, and measured way of talking identify him long before he says his name. Once you get past the cosmetics, however, Joe is committed to his clients. He never fails to follow up, even when it involves a trivial issue. He remembers small matters others overlook. Joe is successful because he never tries to please people with insincere words. He is successful because he takes who he is and uses those characteristics to meet every need his clients might have. Joe's success demonstrates the importance not only of focusing upon the needs of others, but of just being who you are, no frills.

Being yourself is the starting point toward success. Let's take a look at two other examples of how significance-based behavior can increase your sales effectiveness.

June was a secretary in a large sales office. Over the years, she began to notice differences between the behavior of top performing salespeople and low performers. To better understand the differences, she decided to keep an activities calendar on the entire sales force. The results were revealing.

Top performers did one thing that low performers did not: they had a relationship strategy. Top performers focused on lunches, golf games, tennis, etc., with both clients and potential clients. Top performers also spent about half their time maintaining relationships with current accounts and the other half in developing relationships with potential accounts.

A few years later we applied these principles to a project in an entirely different professional area. A three-year-old law firm formed by eight lawyers asked us to look into some of its internal problems. The firm had been structured with one attorney serving as internal administrator and the other seven bringing in clients.

Our opening session revealed the firm's foremost problem was that the seven lawyers were not bringing in enough business to support the budget. We decided to work with the attorneys to help them focus on their weekly schedule and increase the time they spent with potential clients. Each one listed his hobbies, lunch plans, and other activities, and agreed to begin trying to schedule at least two activities per week with a potential client.

Seven members of the firm gave the plan little more than lip service; the only one who tackled it aggressively was the office administrator. Within six months, he was the highest billing attorney in the office. This made him realize the others were not putting out the effort to build the practice—so he left and started his own firm.

Ironically, prior to his training, the administrator-attorney lacked self-confidence. He chose to be come the administrator because he didn't think he could successfully practice law. Later he told us that learning to spend time on relationships had changed not only his career, but his view of himself. He realized he did have what it takes to excel in his own law practice.

## The Four Ps of Selling

A number of years ago, Dave Rettig and his partner faced a problem. They had acquired a business that seemed to be doing well, except for one thing. Neither of them had any sales background yet they continually had to train their sales force.

All the training programs they investigated were just too expensive, so they decided to apply their entrepreneurial skills to their problem. Studying the top sales approaches used by major companies, they took the best parts of each one and combined them into an easy, yet effective, sales model for their own group. The result of their work was the 4P sales approach.[1]

One advantage of the 4P model is its simplicity. Another advantage is how quickly it enables a person to begin selling. Since it is easily remembered, it becomes an excellent reference or framework for sales trainers working with new salespeople in the field. *The entire approach is based upon listening.*

Before we explore the 4Ps, let's underscore a major point. People who believe in their own significance know they have something to offer. More than offering a product or a service, they are offering themselves. They know that as they invest personal energy into their efforts, the covert message will get through, "You are important to me. My priority is to know and help you." That is the common thread in each of the illustrations presented so far in this chapter.

When most people buy a product or a service, they wonder, *Who is this person I'm doing business with?* They want to know they are spending their time and money wisely, but they also want to know they will be respected in the process.

So what are the four Ps of selling? They are: Person, Probe, Presentation, Profit. Let's take a look at each of them.

## 1. PERSON

The 4P approach begins with a focus on the *person* to whom you are selling. The salesperson begins by asking three or four questions about the customer or decision maker. It is important to establish a sense of genuine regard for the individual, to pick up tidbits about the person from observing what surrounds him or her. Do trophies, plaques, or other personal recognition items indicate a special interest? For instance:

- I see from the diploma on the wall that you went to Boston University. How did you like studying there?

- That is a nice trophy on your shelf. Did you lead the team that won it?

- How long have you been with the firm?

- Just exactly what does your job entail?

You need to know with whom you are dealing, and specifically how you can enrich his or her life through your services. Knowing little things about the person can help you become a significance builder.

An insurance executive once explained, "My greatest drawback in selling is that I don't have a hard product to show potential customers—you know, something tangible. In a sense, I'm selling something abstract. The way to break through that barrier is to remind the customer that I'm focused on who he is. I need to know little things about him so I can tailor-make a product that will meet his needs. No two people have the exact same circumstances. I want to create a relaxed atmosphere where we can get to know each other."

A representative for a pharmaceutical company noticed a commendation the pharmacist had received from a local children's charity. "Looks like you put in some extra time each week at the clothing bank for children," he commented. "I'll bet you've had some heartwarming experiences." With that, the pharmacist told of several families she had helped through her volunteer work. Her enthusiasm bubbled over and she was pleased to know he had a genuine interest in her story. He summarized the discussion

*At the heart of success in selling is
the ability to put others' needs
before your own.*

by saying, "It really makes my day to know I'm working with someone who genuinely cares about people in a hands-on way."

Later when the pharmacist commented on why she recommended the rep's products, she explained, "I like working with someone who cares about people, just as I do. I know he's doing more than just a job."

By connecting with the person, you affirm that you are doing more than performing a job. Rather, you are building significance and contributing to the greater good of that person's world.

## 2. PROBE

The probe also involves asking several lead-in questions. Note that the transition from the person to the probe is quite natural, since the salesperson continues to ask questions and listens. The probe might go like this:

- What does your current vendor do that you really like?

- What do you look for in a vendor?

- Can you give me some idea of what is most important in your purchasing decision?

The questions obviously lead to other questions. As the prospective client gives answers, the salesperson begins to understand what the customer is looking for. More importantly, the customer is telling you how he or she wants to be helped.

Notice an important ingredient in this phase. While probing, you are not thinking, *How can I manipulate you to buy what I want you to buy?* Instead, the thought is, *What needs do you have and how can I help?*

The successful salesperson is not looking for the quick buck. Many salespeople can master the techniques of forcing a close on a customer, but this represents only a short-term "score." By committing to the significance principle, salespeople are more focused on the long-term. Rather than worrying about making today's quota, they are concerned instead with meeting the customer's unique set of needs.

## 3. PRESENTATION

As we explore this "P," consider this: *Canned presentations tell your customers you think they are DIRT.* If you are unwilling to listen to prospective customers and design your sales presentation around their needs, you do not deserve to be in sales. That is why the customer's comments, and nothing more, must be allowed to design the sales presentation. If the salesperson is tuned in, he or she will be listening at all four levels of communication.

A friend learned this lesson on a hospital sales call a few years ago. The purchasing manager freely shared her expectations of a supplier. Their conversation was open except when she referred to her current supplier. At those times she lowered her eyes to the right and talked in a softer voice. The salesman eventually found a polite way to ask about their current supplier. "Look," she replied, "I hate our current supplier—but he's my boss's brother-in-law. I don't have a choice in who I buy from."

"Seems to me that you have a politically delicate situation here," the salesman said, "so I'll just stick to the facts of what I can do for you, then you can decide how you'll handle it from there."

He then showed her his product line and went over prices, ordering, and shipment procedures. The purchasing agent seemed relieved that he did not pressure her, and in gratitude she committed to bring in his products slowly so the hospital staff could see for themselves their benefits. Over the next months, she became a loyal customer of the firm.

Proactive listening can go a long way toward helping you understand the customer's expectations. It was this salesman's ability to listen that enabled him to get to the real issues in his call. The presentation should reflect the salesperson's proactive listening. To put it another way, throughout the sales call the salesperson should make a personal list of the customer's perceived needs so that those items will be addressed in the presentation. The presentation must address each of those issues.

Here is the exciting part: If you make your list as you listen, the presentation becomes little more than addressing the issues important to the customer. As you focus upon being a proactive listener and respond to the stated and perceived needs of the customer, you affirm his or her significance.

Remember, the 4P approach is all about listening and asking questions. Except for the points you make in your presentation, all you do is ask customer-focused questions. In closing the call, that is exactly what you continue to do—ask questions.

## 4. PROFIT

We do not like to call this part of a sales call the "close." We think the idea of profit fits best the desired result of a good sales call—both parties profit. Simply put, the profit part of the call is where you confirm that you understand the customer's needs and your offer meets those needs precisely. Here are some typical profit questions:

- In your opinion, does our product meet all the needs you have shared with me?

- Are there any areas where you still have some doubts about our product or our service?

- Are there any remaining barriers that might keep you from ordering our product?

The conversation differs with each product, but the idea remains the same. Throughout the call, you have been careful not to put the customer in a corner or create an uncomfortable climate. At this point you might ask an "action" question such as, "Do you feel like you are ready to go ahead and order your first batch?" If the answer is yes, you complete the call in two ways:

1. You give instructions on how to order (or take the order).
2. You make an appointment to call on them at some future time to assess their satisfaction with the product.

This is a simplified version of the 4P model adapted for selling; it serves as a skeleton or framework for an expanded version of the 4P model. You can use it to become productive in a short period of time. That is certainly what Sue did.

We were conducting a one-day sales seminar for a group of office supplies franchisees across the United States. At one stop, Sue, the wife of one of the franchisees, came to a seminar. At the end of the day she decided the model was so simple, she was going to try it.

She did so, and both she and her husband were astounded by her success. Understand, not only had she never sold anything before, she was petrified at the thought of making a sales call. Yet the very first day she enjoyed great success and continued to be successful for a long time.

Before this she thought of herself as shy and never imagined she could be a good salesperson. She discovered how rapidly people warmed up to her when she started asking questions about them. From that point forward, it wasn't a sales call, it was a relationship founded upon significance building that made selling enjoyable (as well as beneficial to her).

Selling and customer service have a lot in common. In fact, the principles are so similar we would like to briefly describe a successful customer service approach that has endured the test of time.

## The American Airlines Customer Service Model

Years ago American Airlines devised a checklist for its customer service agents that serves as a simple model for significance-building transactions with the public. Notice the strong focus upon the customer in this model. The customer service "scoring" factors in the model are as follows:

- Did you smile at the customer? (for airport personnel)

- Did you make eye contact?

- Did you use the customer's name?

- Did you clearly understand the customer's needs?

- Did you review everything you did to be sure it was what the customer wanted?

- Did you thank the customer for their business and use their name to close the conversation?

We recently visited a major national bank and used this simple checklist to measure the bank's level of customer service. If the employee accomplished four of six items, we scored an "effective customer contact." Based on that criteria, less than 30 percent of the customer contacts could be rated as effective!

Let's put our "significance" glasses on and take a look at both the 4P selling approach and the American Airlines approach.

Both of these approaches tell us that we must understand how to make the customer the most important aspect of every transaction. The bank we informally studied was saying to their customers a whopping 70 percent of the time, "You are not very important to us."

The issue in life, in business, or in society, is our ability to recognize the underlying significance needs of others. We must understand that a sales transaction is far more than that. It is a *person-to-person* transaction. If we view it as a sales transaction alone, we will ultimately lose. The same is true in life or business. If you are unable to take your eyes off of your own need for significance and replace it with others' need for significance, you will inevitably fail.

But why fail? You don't need to. Choose to live out the significance principle, and watch your sales grow. We bet you'll like it.

## SELLING IS A SIGNIFICANCE TRANSACTION

- *The next time someone tries to sell you something, look at their sales approach and test it against the 4P model.*

- *When you go to a bank or other service organization, grade the treatment you received against the American Airlines model.*

- *If you work with a volunteer organization, audit your customer contact quality to see if you are a customer-oriented organization.*

- *If you work at an office, observe the selling or customer service activities. Try to identify areas where improvement would significantly enhance customer retention.*

- *Regardless of where you work in an organization, spend a few hours with a salesperson. Evaluate their effectiveness by comparing it with the 4P model (no criticism allowed).*

- *If you are stopped by a police officer, evaluate the officer's "customer focus" based upon what you have learned in this chapter. (Police officers call this "community policing" and it is becoming an important part of the work in many police departments.)*

# *Chapter* Twelve
## PUTTING IT ALL TOGETHER

On September 16, 1892, Ida May Elliot was born. At the age of ten she and her two siblings lost their mother to tuberculosis, and she was forced to mature quickly. As she aged and touched the lives of many, she became known to everyone as "Mom," daily demonstrating her "can-do" spirit and her enthusiasm for life.

Born in the small town of Morely, Colorado, Ida May moved through the Southwest as her father helped establish Santa Fe train depots in the remote regions of Colorado, New Mexico, and Kansas. She learned to use the telegraph by age five, and through her friendships with local children became proficient in Spanish. When Ida May was just eight, her baby sister got tuberculosis, and since her mother was ill with the same disease, the task of caretaking fell to her and her brother, Edgar. The baby died, and after her mother also passed away, Ida May became caretaker for the rest of the family, assuming all the tasks formerly tackled by her mother. Not one to complain, Ida May accepted her role willingly and even helped her dad manage the train station. She also tutored some of the local Hispanic kids and was especially effective because she could explain the lessons in both English and Spanish.

The depot in New Mexico had little living area, so one day her dad suggested that she and her friends spruce up an old box car on the side track and make a bedroom out of it. So they did! While not airtight, the box car was cozy enough. Mom thought of it as a luxury because now she had her own room and lots of extra space for her friends.

Early in her adult years, the harsh winter of 1918 produced a worldwide influenza epidemic and her small community was not spared. Mom and some of the other railroad workers who also lived in boxcars were the only ones who did not get sick. The only doctor in town was so ill he could not care for anyone, so Mom willingly tended to anyone who needed it. First, she obtained clean beds for the sick, putting them in tents if no other place was available. Every day they made large pots of soup to distribute to the community. Working around the clock, Mom and her fellow workers took turns grabbing naps whenever they could.

As the years passed, Mom became station master at Berino, New Mexico—the first woman ever to achieve that position. Mom remained single until she was thirty. Several years after marrying, she entered the restaurant business in Los Lunas, New Mexico, and her caring reputation soon made her restaurant into the hangout for high school kids. She often went the extra mile for her customers, like the time the entire football team showed up at closing time to celebrate a victory. Instead of shooing them away, she cooked a celebration dinner all by herself. The kids were so thrilled they cleaned up the place for her. Apparently they thought she was their Mom too.

Eventually Mom closed the restaurant and went to work in the school cafeteria until her retirement at age seventy. Barbara

Medlin, one of her granddaughters, remembers helping Mom with her cooking preparations early in the morning. Though she was still just a preschooler, Barbara was Mom's little sidekick who helped count giant cans of vegetables and sort pinto beans. Ever patient, Mom never let on that such a small child was in the way. Mom was the ultimate significance builder.

A rocking chair did not suit Mom in her retirement, so she became a volunteer for the New Mexico School for Retarded Children. One of her first assignments was Lynn, a six-year-old boy placed at the school immediately after birth. Considered severely retarded, Lynn also suffered from Ruthmund-Thompson Syndrome, a disease that caused him to age ten years every year. Although he was chronologically six, physically he was sixty and mentally two or three. Mom was told he couldn't be expected to live beyond age eight. Lynn was not toilet trained, nor could he feed or dress himself, and his vocabulary amounted to three words. A few wild sprigs of hair sprouted over his otherwise bald head, cataracts covered his eyes, and his skin wrinkled and cracked. School officials gave Mom the opportunity to refuse working with Lynn, believing that the task would be both physically and emotionally taxing. Mom turned them down and gladly accepted the challenge.

Mom saw it as her privilege to love Lynn. While daily feeding him, changing his diaper, and caring for his physical needs, she gave him the affection he had been missing his entire life. Through Mom's patience and persistence, Lynn eventually needed no more diapers. He learned to dress and feed himself. He even learned to communicate, thus wildly surpassing everyone's expectations—except Mom's.

When Lynn surpassed the school's criteria for remaining an inpatient, and since his parents had turned him over to the state, Mom petitioned to take him into her own home as a foster child.

She enrolled him in school and every day Lynn caught the bus at the top of Mom's country road. When he was home, Lynn ran to greet any car that came by, taking each visitor by the hand and proudly leading them inside. Lynn's enthusiasm and appearance startled new visitors, but "regulars" knew Lynn's greeting was part of the visit. He mimicked the giving of love and affection that Mom showed him.

At age nineteen—eleven years past his life expectancy—Lynn suffered a stroke and died. Thanks to Mom, his later years were of highest quality.

Mom was publicly acclaimed many times for her courage and care for others. She received many awards, including a special recognition by President Reagan for her work with handicapped children. She worked at the school until a stroke sidelined her at age ninety.

She spent her last few years in a wheelchair, but she was still Mom. At age ninety-eight, Mom's family was called to her hospital room to pay their last respects. One grandchild who had been especially close to Mom entered the room and began crying. He sobbed because he knew he was about to lose someone who had cared dearly for him, someone who meant the world to him. A voice from the bed interrupted his tears. "Honey, what can I do for you?" It was Mom, still true to her character.

Later that day, she died.

Mom's life epitomized how people can find their own significance by actively touching the lives of others. We want to say more about Mom and people like her, but first we want to tell a story about the other side of significance.

## Significance at the Expense of Others

Susan Rockford was excited about her new position at the Eagle National Bank (a fictitious name). Susan, a highly ethical person, had been told the bank's management and staff shared her commitment and she delighted in the opportunity to work with such a team. The bank often ran ads about its commitment to family values, integrity, and patriotism, and such public pronouncements weighed heavily in her decision to take a job there.

Susan's first day on the job was like most first days . . . until a loan officer spoke with her about working at ENB. "Susan," he said, "There's one thing you have to remember if you are going to survive at ENB."

"What's that?" she wondered.

"You must never forget that this is a kingdom, and Everett Watson (the CEO of the bank) and Margarite Mayer (the controller) are royalty. Everett is the king and Margarite is the queen. If you ever forget that, you're in serious trouble. If you remember that in everything you say and do, you will do quite well here."

The statement perplexed her, but Susan decided not to pursue it. Soon, however, she discovered what he meant. Everett's wife had been an invalid for many years and the bank seemed to be his life, his outlet for personal stress. While amicable and pleasant on the outside, Everett demanded total obedience in every detail. Those who surrounded him enforced his wishes. Margarite was a lot like Everett and focused upon carrying out his every wish. At the same time, she appeared to exert great influence over him (but never contradicted him).

A hyper-controller, Everett decided what supplies should be ordered for the bank, even for the bathroom. It was easy for him to do, since everyone around him made sure they passed every decision by him. Ditto the loan officers. Each loan, regardless of its size, passed through Everett. His ferocious temper reminded everyone to steer clear of his bad side.

Everett grew up poor but decided to identify with the old money group in Kansas City, where the bank was located. He nearly drooled over his most high profile customers, but if you weren't upper crust, he held you in contempt. When new employees joined the bank, Everett at first made them feel like necessary additions to the team—but it didn't take long to realize the honeymoon would be short-lived if they did not learn to think as he did. Anita Winn realized this problem quickly.

Anita was one of a number of assistants who worked directly with Everett. Her reputation for efficiency led ENB to hire her away from a competing bank. She loved the job at first and committed to becoming an exceptional employee.

But it didn't take long for her to realize that Everett had given her a much higher than average salary—not because of her exceptional skills, but so she would find it difficult to leave. It seemed that every project she did became the object of endless corrections and criticism. In spite of it all, Anita never said anything to anyone. She never complained or lowered her work standards, nor did she try to talk behind Everett's back. Fellow employees recognized her as one of the bank's top performers and assumed she was very pleased to be by Everett's side.

One day, however, Anita walked up to Susan and asked to speak with her. "I know you've only been here a few weeks, but I just have to blow off some steam," she said. "I feel as if you're the only friend I have at the bank, even though you've been here for such a short time."

"Let's get a cup of coffee," responded Susan, "and you can tell me all about it."

Anita unraveled the painful history of her two years at the bank. She told of the contempt Margarite had showed her. She recounted incident after incident in which Everett demeaned her work, her appearance, and everything about her. "I told him I found another job and would be leaving in two weeks," she said. "He fired me on the spot. And if that weren't enough, Margarite was in my office less than ten minutes later, telling me how incompetent I was and that I was dispensable. This has all been a horrible experience."

Susan's next few years echoed those of Anita. She found it ironic that Everett's cronies raved about what a fine man he was and that the other employees also talked about what a great man he was. She also found it ironic that Everett publicly portrayed himself in a positive light, while behind the scenes he was exactly the opposite.

Susan lasted almost three years at the bank. After a number of conflicts over ethical issues with both Everett and Margarite, she finally decided she could take no more. Like Anita, she resigned and took another job at another bank. And still Everett continued his ways, oblivious to the raft of disgruntled employees he was creating.

## Putting It All Together

It's easy to see the differences between Mom and Everett, isn't it? Mom lived to affirm the significance of others, while Everett and Margarite built their own significance at the expense of others.

Whether you are at the bottom of an organization, the middle, or the top, you have a decision to make about your own significance. Like everyone else, you long to feel significant—but you must decide how you will acquire that significance. Whether you are the chairman of a multinational corporation or a customer service agent for an airline, you have to answer one question: Will I be a Mom or an Everett?

It's time to evaluate yourself. If you are a "taker," like Everett, are you willing to commit to actively recognize the significance of others? On the other hand, if you are a significance builder, like Mom, are you willing to sustain your commitment to build others up? That is the challenge you face today and for the rest of your life.

With that in mind, allow us to offer a few closing thoughts on applying the principles of this book. Let's briefly consider both personal and organizational issues as they relate to the significance principle.

## The Significance Principle: A Personal Perspective

Many books that discuss behavior lack a practical dimension. They leave open the question, "Does the approach I just learned work in the real world?"

We honestly admit that the significance approach is no cure-all. In fact, there are times when it will seem to have no effect at all.

For example, let's reexamine the story about Susan Rockford. Personalities like Everett, the bank CEO, often attract associates with the same problems of insecurity they display. We call this "corporate codependency."

Susan discovered that one of her subordinates often suffered extreme mood swings. The worker's behavior became so bizarre that it began to affect Susan's attitude. To further add to the problem, the subordinate's best friend was—you guessed it—Margarite. Susan found herself trapped in *One Flew over the Cuckoo's Nest*.

A visit with a psychologist confirmed that Susan's subordinate displayed clear indications of psychological dysfunction. The specialist explained that the subordinate was incapable of dealing rationally with people. The bottom line—no matter what Susan

*Deceit may win a few battles,*
*but integrity wins*
*on the battlefield of life.*

did, no matter how much she tried to build up her subordinate, Susan would be unable to change her behavior in any way. It was something clearly beyond her control. It was then Susan decided to resign her position.

You may face similar issues. Recall our chapter on anger. Did you recognize similar behaviors in anyone you know? If you did, you may also conclude that you are unable to deal with people at the extreme ends of dysfunctional behavior. For that reason we want to reemphasize the principle of disconnection. Recognize that you will never be able to change some situations. Once you discover yourself in a situation like Susan's, you need to disconnect from the psychological games long enough to find an exit. We cannot emphasize this enough.

Consider a high-level executive, prone to write caustic and cold letters. Each time an associate or subordinate challenges him he responds, "That's just the way I test out on the Meyers-Briggs. That's the way I am."

To that we reply, "Bunk!"

> LASTING CHANGE BEGINS WITH YOU. CHOOSE TO BEGIN A
> LIFE-ENHANCING JOURNEY TO EXCELLENCE OF LIFE.

Just like anyone else, he has the ability to change; but he must first decide he *wants* to change. It is simply wrong to say that we cannot change our behavior.

> THE PEOPLE YOU WANT TO CHANGE, YOU MUST FIRST RESPECT .
> . . AND THEY MUST KNOW THAT YOU RESPECT THEM.

True change can happen, but at its foundation must be the personal humility to examine oneself with honesty and integrity. It is wrong to constantly engage in conflicts with others while maintaining that *others* must change. Change begins with the willingness to tell *ourselves* the truth about *ourselves*.

At least 99 percent of the time, the people who seek counseling or consulting want to know how to change *others*. Yet much of the time it is the person seeking the consultation who needs the change.

The significance paradox states that we find our own significance by building up the significance of others. And that can happen only when we discover that we can never change others by tearing them down; it occurs only when we commit to be a positive presence in their lives. If you want to help change others for the better, the journey begins with you. You must choose to recognize the significance of others, and this choice must become a lifelong commitment.

> ### The Significance Paradox
> THE WAY TO FIND YOUR OWN SIGNIFICANCE
> IS TO ACTIVELY RECOGNIZE THE SIGNIFICANCE OF OTHERS.

# The Significance Principle: An Organizational Perspective

As we recently assessed a major organization—one of the oldest companies in the United States—we tried not to show our concern about the enormous performance gaps we identified. The gaps suggested that decades of success had allowed this world-renowned organization to decay into a bureaucracy that defied any attempt to effect positive change.

We first told the firm's representative that these performance gaps probably would significantly impact future revenues. "They already have," he responded. "We are experiencing a steady decline in revenues, and those of us who understand the issues cannot seem to get management at higher levels to listen to us."

Then he said the organization had become highly political with many turf battles keeping management busy fighting each other instead of solving problems.

"You are right again," he responded. "I can't get two of our major divisions to talk with each other about cooperating, even though it's obvious that teamwork is the only way to solve these problems."

We also suggested that the hyper-controlling approach of management, coupled with a culture that rejected most aspects of change, inhibited future opportunities. Yet if these barriers were removed, we thought the firm could grow 200 percent in a fairly short period of time.

"I agree," he said. "We have concluded that short-term revenue growth could even be in the 300 percent range—if we can drive empowerment into the organization."

It's one thing to know the truth; it's quite another to put it into practice. Truth dismissed or unused is no different from falsehood. In the end, either one can kill you.

The link between management culture and profit has been understood for a long time. What has been missing is assessment instruments that measure how people treat others. We have spent the last eighteen months designing and testing instruments that measure transactions of this nature, and we have been encouraged by the performance of those instruments. Yet our approach is radical in that we want to make people in organizations accountable for how they treat others.

Organizations that truly want to maximize profit and performance must understand that *high organizational performance begins with treating people right.* And if this doesn't begin with the CEO, it can never be effective. If this sounds too simple, remember the bottom line: *There is a direct link between how you treat people (significance issues) and the profitability of the firm.* All too often, senior managers give lip service to the idea of "empowerment," only to remind their subordinates how unimportant they are. We are talking about money . . . profit . . . incentives . . . profit sharing. It all starts at the top, and we are convinced that if those at the top become accountable to the real driver of profit—empowerment, intellectual capital—then the organization's performance will skyrocket.

Remember Mom? What do you think Mom would have done had she found herself in the middle of a cumbersome bureaucracy? What would she have tried if she needed to make a change from the bottom or even the middle of the organization? You know as well as we do that Mom would find a way, no matter what the odds, to build significance-enhancing behavior into the organization. She would start with herself first, then she would find ways to convince others of the possibilities.

What about you?

If you are in an organization, no doubt you can see the possibilities of applying the significance principle among your colleagues. In fact, you can probably give us specifics about how implementing the principle as a corporate way of life could change your organization.

That is our challenge to you. Change begins with you. Change begins with how you treat others and your willingness to build significance into the lives of others. Once you commit to living a significance-building life, you can positively affect the lives of those around you. Ultimately, you may be able to affect your entire organization.

## Make the Commitment!

We want to close with two summaries that we believe encapsulate our book. Use them as your personal commitment to your family, your friends, and your associates at work. They'll be glad you did . . . and so will you.

## FIVE RELATIONSHIP VALUES OF SIGNIFICANCE-BUILDING PEOPLE

1. *They actively seek to discover the value in others and are able to overlook their shortcomings.*

2. *They avoid even the appearance of self-importance.*

3. *They want significance building to become their way of life.*

4. *They are committed to being people of character and integrity.*

5. *They are committed to excellence in everything they do.*

## FIVE RELATIONSHIP VALUES OF SIGNIFICANCE-BUILDING LEADERS

1. *They value the significance of others in their organization, regardless of their position or title.*

2. *They measure their personal success by the success of their subordinates.*

3. *They are team members and coaches; they lead by example and not by directive.*

4. *They are proactive listeners who follow through.*

5. *They consider their personal morals, integrity, and character as the most important aspects of their persona.*

# Chapter *Thirteen*
# THE TEN VALUES OF HIGH PERFORMANCE ORGANIZATIONS AND HIGH PERFORMANCE PEOPLE

Interviews conducted for this book uncovered two important issues. First, "high performance people"—that is, workers who perform exceptionally because of their great relationships with others—tend to practice certain values. Second, organizations that perform at a high level over a long term tend to foster management approaches and internal cultures that focus upon the same values.

Based on our investigation into both areas, we developed our "Ten Values of Significance Builders."

It has been said that who you are on the inside becomes how you are on the outside. We developed our ten values with that in mind. The truth is, we live out our values in our relationships. So as you read about our personal experiences and observations, we challenge you not to look at the outside of your activities, but to the inside. Only when you change your internal values will your external transactions build high performance relationships.

In this final chapter we would like to do something a little different. Each of us will share some personal stories about people we know or company situations we have observed. In order to communicate the real value of the people we are writing about, we will tell these stories in the first person.

# 1. They Practice Humility

(Jim's comments)

Over the past fifteen years I had the opportunity to get to know Bill Mitchell, the recently retired vice chairman of Texas Instruments. I met Bill after joining a family-type club west of Dallas, Texas. I enjoyed visiting with him; he is one of those down-to-earth people who just make you feel comfortable.

Bill and Mary, his wife, had a small cottage on the property, as did Patsy, my wife, and I. We socialized on a number of occasions but Bill almost never talked about what he did. Even when he did so, he never talked about his title or responsibilities. In fact, he was so humble about his work that I would not have been surprised to discover he was an engineer.

As time went on, I figured Bill probably had a pretty responsible job. Later I realized he actually had very high-level responsibilities. Now, I've never known anyone who held a high-level position who, at one point or another, didn't at least drop a hint about the importance of his work or position . . . until I met Bill. After knowing Bill for years, I finally figured out that he led one of the firm's largest divisions and was integrally involved in some of our country's top defense projects. Yet even after Bill was promoted to vice chairman, he was still Bill. He returned my calls. He was the same, humble Bill I had always known.

I discovered Bill treated everyone the same way. Jeanne, his administrative assistant, once said that he "treated me like I was a really important person." Another subordinate also commented, "He's just about the finest man I've ever worked with."

And how did Bill see himself? He finally slipped one day after his 1997 retirement when we were talking about his former position as vice chairman. "I'm just a simple engineer," he said.

I couldn't help but laugh. That really did not describe Bill! Bill is an accomplished executive, a highly successful manager, a man who has been involved in some of the most leading-edge technological developments of this century. Yet his comment—"I'm just a simple engineer"—revealed to me why Bill had been so successful.

Bill, a truly confident and accomplished man, never allowed phenomenal success to change one of his bedrock values: humility.

## 2. They Proactively Focus on Others

(Les's comments)

At age forty-two, Deb Vickery had everything going her way. The mother of two teenage girls and the wife of a successful businessman—as well as a part-time fitness instructor and a part-time development officer for a private school—she never lacked for things to do.

One day she found a lump near her collar bone. An appointment with her doctor confirmed her worst fears: Yes, it was abnormal; yes, it would have to be surgically removed; (and later) yes, it was malignant.

Bewildered and afraid the first few days after getting the news, Deb spent hours discussing her illness with family, close friends, and her minister. Time was of the essence, since the cancer had spread into her lymph glands. Deb needed a personal coping plan.

Through the next few months Deb endured chemotherapy, then radiation. Yet despite the side effects of hair loss, extreme fatigue, nausea, and frequent stomach cramps, Deb describes that segment of her life as one of her finest.

Finest? How could that be? Everything that had kept her energized was now disrupted; how could anyone call it one of the "best times"?

Deb could do so because as she drew strength from her many well-wishers, she discovered she had been placed in a unique position to give strength back. As she displayed courage and faith, she realized that the same strength and goodness could be found in others. She did not deny her own needs and frustrations, yet she welcomed the many opportunities to minister to those who imagined they had come to minister to her.

She stayed focused on others, even though she had ample reasons to let the focus remain on her. For instance, on her last day of chemo treatment, an elderly patient at the cancer clinic stopped by her cubicle and said, "Whenever I see you here, you seem so willing to be helpful with the nurses, and you are such an encourager to everyone around you."

How could anyone be an encourager in such circumstances? Deb explained that through her faith she believed she could endure her ordeal and in the meantime, she could be a beacon to guide others with similar struggles. No wonder the same elderly patient later said, "I need the same faith that you have."

Another time a friend, Arlene, visited Deb at home. In the course of conversation she mentioned how stressful her family-owned business was. After a lengthy discussion, Arlene said what so many others had found to be true in their visits with Deb: "I came to cheer her, but I'm the one who has benefited the most."

Near the end of a meeting at her church, a woman Deb did not know declared, "Before we go, I want to say how thankful I am for Deb Vickery. For the last three months I've been watching her from a distance, and I've been genuinely touched by the kind and gentle spirit she has shown in the midst of her own trials." This woman was enduring her own medical difficulties and explained that she had gained a greater sense of optimism after observing Deb's ability to focus on others.

What does Deb say about all of this? "I've realized that my suffering has caused me to be at the center of a lot of attention, so I have learned to view this as an opportunity to convey just how appreciative I am of others," she says. "With the increased spotlight on me, it just means I have an increased ability to give of myself in ways that will encourage others."

As I have watched Deb go through all of this, I, too, have been encouraged. More than that, Deb has learned well one of life's most important lessons: By choosing to proactively focus on others, her own sense of significance has soared.

## 3. They Practice Integrity

(Les and Jim)

A renowned offshore sailboat racer faced an ethical issue hundreds of miles from shore. Offshore racers often get separated by weather and sail miles apart. In one race, the boat piloted by the renowned sailor accidentally hit a buoy set apart as a turning point for the race. Rules stipulate that whoever hits a buoy must sail by it and go around it again. For a fifty or sixty-foot sailboat in heavy seas, this can be a difficult and long task.

"Forget it!" shouted a crewman. "There's not another boat within twenty miles of us. Keep on going! No one will ever know." The quiet voice from the helm said just two words before giving the command to turn the boat around, "I would."

People of integrity never worry about who is watching or who isn't. People of integrity don't have two sets of rules, one for public occasions and one for private. People of integrity never change their values, regardless of the price. Without integrity, there can be no trust. And without trust, people cannot be built up.

## 4. They Deal Positively with Conflict

(Les and Jim)

Ann Beal was an eager, young software engineer in the mid 1980s when General Motors bought Electronic Data Systems. Once the sale was completed, she was assigned to the Detroit office to teach a group of auto design engineers how to use the EDS software, which was quite different from what they had previously used. With her customary vigor she approached the job with all the energy she could muster. She tried making her presentations informative and was open to give individual instructions so her all-male group could soon get up to speed.

One major unanticipated problem quickly emerged. The men simply did not like her presence. She learned that they felt uncertain about the personal implications of the merger of the two companies and they resented that this young, perky woman was going to tell them what they were supposed to do. Ann was naturally offended at their rebuff and she was in a major quandary: "What do I do with this large of a conflict?"

One of her mentors, Harold, pulled her aside and explained, "Ann, you've come into this group of men with loads of ideas and information, but before they can accept your instructions, they need to accept you. Show them your heart."

Not entirely sure what this meant, she determined nonetheless to look for openings to break the logjam. The next day at lunch, she noticed that one of the engineers, Mike, was eating homemade chocolate chip cookies. Recalling fond memories of her mom's homemade cookies, she told him, "I've always been willing to let everyone else eat the cookies when they were served

*Transparency is integrity
and honesty revealed.*

because I'd much prefer to eat the dough." They laughed and she thought nothing more of it.

The next day, Mike again was eating his chocolate chip cookies, but additionally he brought a lump of cookie dough for Ann. She, of course, laughed and consumed it gladly, not realizing that this would become the beginning of her breakthrough. "Over the next days and weeks, I found it easier to get to know something personal about each man in my group," she explains. "It's odd, but as soon as they saw me as a regular human, their resistance to me decreased greatly."

What did Ann learn? Conflict can be naturally built into any work setting, especially when major changes are in the works. "People don't like feeling that someone is just going to barge into their world, telling them how they've got to alter what they are used to doing," Ann reflects. "And if you push your agenda too powerfully you're bound to get resistance, just as I did. In the midst of conflict or challenges or change, people want first to know that you see them in the human dimension. You've got to get on their level and let them know that you care about them."

## 5. They Live the Significance Paradox

(Les and Jim)

Ron Haake is a sales manager for AT&T Business Markets in Ft. Worth, Texas. In September 1993, Ron was asked to move from his assignment in Dallas to take other responsibilities in Ft. Worth. The new group had the lowest performance in the office.

Ron used a five-prong approach to lead his team to enhanced performance:

1. Communicate expectations, then coach people to performance expectations.

2. Establish a clear understanding of progress ("How am I doing?").
3. Recognize accomplishments:
   • On the spot
   • As a team
   • In the presence of the entire branch (public ceremony)
4. Teamwork is the key to success.
5. Focus on team needs: family, personal, professional.

Ron viewed himself as a member of the team, not as a superior. "I'm not a control freak," he says. "I work as a member of our team and coach them so that they can succeed. If I help each member of the team, then we all win as a team."

How did Ron achieve success? "I think the turnaround for this team was when they realized that I genuinely viewed my job in terms of helping them achieve success," he said. "Isn't that what management really should be all about? If I coerce my team into achieving a goal, I might get recognition, but that would take credit away from the people who actually did the work. That's just not right."

Ron's use of the significance principle has paid off. Consider the results:

• In the first year of Ron's leadership, the team moved from the bottom of the performance ratings to the middle.

• In 1995 they became the top performing team in the branch.

• In 1996 they were #1 again.

• In 1997 they ended the year in a battle for #1.

Since 1994, Ron has been twice-recognized by AT&T's Leaders Council; only the top 2 percent of salespeople in the firm receive this award. Since Ron took the helm in 1994, another change has taken place. The team has decided that it wants to make all of the hiring decisions, a decision Ron whole-heartedly approves. And there is more. The separate members have come together as a team and realize they depend upon each other for success. "My team makes more joint calls than any other team in our branch," says Ron. By helping each other, members of Ron's team not only achieve personal goals, but team goals as well.

Ron credits a former manager for much of his success. "Beverly Wilburn taught me a lot," he said. "She is committed to excellence, expresses her appreciation for the work of others, and supports them with all of her ability. As a result of working for her, I got to experience firsthand many of the things that help organizations perform. One which stands out is integrity; I believe integrity must be at the center of all communications. Otherwise, there is no trust. When trust is lost, the ability to perform as a team is lost. I learned a lot of those lessons from Beverly."

# 6. They Openly Encourage Others

(Jim)

"Well, I hope you are having an absolutely wonderful day," crackled the old voice on the phone. I never had a problem immediately identifying the speaker: Lucille Middleton. She would ask many questions, listen to my answers, then spend a lot of time encouraging me. Lucille *lived* encouragement. It seemed to be a way of life for her.

I met Lucille at church. At the time, my wife and I were struggling to adopt some really sweet children we met at a children's home. It seemed that at every turn, the people at child protective services would put another roadblock in the way. "I'm going to pray for you, every day," Lucille said to us one day. I didn't know her well at the time, but she sought us out and decided we needed encouragement.

We never succeeded in changing the state's mind about sending the children out-of-state for adoption, but one fantastic benefit came out of our difficulties—I developed a great friend in Lucille.

When we first met, Lucille was in her late seventies. Twice widowed and crippled by rheumatoid arthritis since her forties, she lived her life in constant pain. By her seventh decade of life, she had endured about ten major operations. She was alone and constantly in pain—not exactly a life to envy.

A few years after meeting Lucille, I took a position at a bank. I loved my job and had the opportunity to be promoted to a great position in lending. I remember looking forward to going to work every day—until I learned of problems between the two senior officers and some of the directors. The root of the problem: questionable business practices. It wasn't long before one of the senior officers left. The president of the bank brought in his wife to work as his secretary, and that is when we began to be encouraged to take some ethical shortcuts—especially to misrepresent documentation seen by the bank examiners.

As one of the remaining officers, I was put in a difficult situation, for I was unwilling to cut any corners. This brought down on me the wrath not only of the president, but also his wife. It was perhaps one of the most difficult six months of my life.

Except for my buddy Lucille! Whenever I reached the end of my patience on yet another issue, the phone seemed to ring, and again that crackly old voice would say, "Well, how are you doing today? I said a special prayer for you today."

Lucille always seemed to call at just the right time, bringing her own special brand of encouragement. And don't think I was the only one she encouraged! As I got to know her better, I discovered that even though her disability kept her at home most of the time, she spent hours each day calling people who needed encouragement. I often marveled that she had the strength to spend so much time encouraging others, when most people in her condition wouldn't think of doing more than focus upon their own problems.

Lucille died a few years ago. Despite her pain and personal loss, Lucille Middleton impacted many lives. She never let anything get in the way of her commitment to live out one of the most important values of her personal character: her commitment to encourage others until her last day on this earth.

I still miss her.

## 7. They Use Ceremony to Recognize Others' Significance

(Les)

Freddie Fossier is known at his company as the ultimate "fix-it" man. The main business at SGS Thomson Microelectronics is the manufacturing of semiconductor chips. The machinery is highly sensitive and must be maintained within very precise guidelines. Each day, Freddie and his team are given a rundown of the machinery glitches and malfunctions to correct and they spend their entire day making sure the manufacturing line runs like clockwork. When the troubleshooting problems seem insurmountable, Freddie steps in. Inevitably, he finds a way to solve the problem.

I once asked, "Freddie, do you ever encounter jealousy because you might seem to show up your coworkers?"

"Oh, not at all," Freddie replied. "We're a team and even when I am the one who figures out how to solve a problem, I always make sure the others get credit for their contributions."

At the end of the day, for example, Freddie makes a point to include the names of team contributors in his reports. Freddie believes his team members really appreciate the formal recognition they get at higher levels of the firm. "People appreciate it when they are written up for doing something right," he explains.

Likewise, when Freddie is publicly praised for his work, he will make sure the team members who were instrumental in diagnosing the problem are recognized. "I make it a point to publicly recognize their contributions and offer my thanks for their contributions to our success," says Freddie.

At group gatherings—where people so often are tempted to talk about their own successes—Freddie sings the praises of coworkers. And his public ceremony is sincere. When he comments about someone else, it's not for his own needs or purposes; it's clear that Freddie's objective is to honestly recognize the significance of others' contributions and personal value.

## 8. They Commit to Personal Accountability

(Les and Jim)

Many times we have heard Dr. Charles Swindoll, president of Dallas Theological Seminary, talk about personal accountability. A number of years ago he was asked to become the senior pastor at a church in southern California, and while there he went from obscurity to international notoriety. Within a few short years his ministry expanded to include a daily radio ministry broadcast internationally.

The author of numerous books, Charles Swindoll achieved goals that others only dream about. His ministry impacted the lives of thousands of people, but Dr. Swindoll realized that with fame comes the temptation to become obsessed with self. To help him counter that temptation he formed a personal accountability group.

On his broadcast he often described how a member of his accountability group would challenge him about a particular area of life. Over the years it became clear that his accountability group was one of the driving forces that kept both his ministry and his life on track. Of course, the challenges from his accountability group often hurt. But to this day, his personal circle of accountability friends help him to focus upon the type of husband, mentor, and leader that he wants to be. He knows that without personal accountability, he'd be in trouble.

## 9. They Actively Work to Right Wrongs

(Les)

Brenda Wood of McKinney, Texas, is an administrative assistant for a large medical practice. Among her many responsibilities she must ascertain the level of insurance coverage carried by each patient, then determine which procedures are covered and to what extent.

"As you might imagine," Brenda says, "I deal with a lot of people each day, and it helps when the patient takes responsibility to know what their insurance coverage is and its implications upon their personal financial situation. Not everyone is pleasant when they have to talk with me about their bill, because sometimes they are wrong in their assumptions about how charges will be paid. At the same time, our office can also make mistakes."

So how does Brenda approach her work so that she is not drawn into battles with frustrated patients? "Well, first I remind myself that these people are here because of problems they did not ask for," she says. "They are ill and distraught, so of course they will consider the whole process a hassle.

"Next, I listen. There is always the possibility that I have made an error, or that I can learn from what the patient is saying. Ninety percent of the time, when a complaining person realizes that I'm trying my hardest to correct a mistake or to understand their problem so I can help, their frustration level drops dramatically."

The emotional pitch of Brenda's voice—gentle and considerate—reveals a lot about Brenda's approach. "Sometimes I have to take on the role of educator," she says. "There are times when the patient doesn't understand how to weave through the quagmire of insurance procedures, so as best as possible I explain how they can do that successfully."

Then she adds, "I'm always open to any feedback or questions. You'd be amazed at how much you can learn when you're willing to receive input. Sometimes people think my job is one big headache, but it's really not. When you approach people with the honest attitude of doing your best to correct a problem, that can become a rewarding experience for both parties. You don't ever get tired of that."

Is it any wonder that Brenda Wood's office manager and staff doctors express high levels of confidence in her? Vickie Gage, the office manager, said it best: "I can rest comfortably each day knowing that Brenda is dealing with our patients. She doesn't rattle easily because she doesn't see a frustrated patient as her adversary. She sees herself as a co-laborer who wants to keep the patient education process flowing. What more could you want?"

Brenda Wood leaves the office most days satisfied. Rather than being drawn into negative confrontations, her openness helps her to actively work to right wrongs. Brenda's attitude turns a difficulty into a joy.

## 10. They Are Committed to Excellence

(Les)

As I was relaxing and mentally mapping out my 1997 Memorial Day activities, I received an early morning phone call. The familiar elderly female voice on the other end was clearly shaken. "Les, this is Evelyn," she said. I knew immediately she had bad news about her brother—my former high school principal and one of my closest friends.

"George has taken a turn for the worse," she continued, "and he's in the intensive care unit. The doctor has told us not to expect him to go home."

George's battle with diabetes had worn out his body and now his kidneys and heart were failing. Evelyn continued, "Are you still going to speak at his funeral when the time comes?"

"Of course I will," I replied.

Over twenty-five years had passed since I moved to Texas from my boyhood home in Atlanta, Georgia, but George Woodruff and I had stayed in close contact throughout the years. We enjoyed many fishing trips together and shared many memories, and whenever I traveled through his part of the country I made a point to stop and spend a day or an evening with him.

Woody (that's what I had called him for years) and I had discussed my speaking at his funeral, but now that the time was upon me, I questioned what I could possibly say to summarize my thoughts about his life. As I sat down to collect my memories, I repeatedly returned to his commitment to excellence. "There's no need trying to tackle a problem," he would tell me, "if you're not going to give it your best. Laziness never got anyone anywhere."

I first encountered George Woodruff in the fall of 1967 as a student entering Lakeshore High School. It did not take me long to realize he was a man who set extremely high standards for his faculty as well as his students. He made it his purpose in life to ensure that everyone around him understood the importance of excellence in every endeavor.

Excellence is contagious. When leaders commit to excellence, as Woody did, it affects the lives of everyone who comes into contact with them. That was certainly true in Woody's life. Year after year, his schools boasted the highest numbers of National Merit Scholars in his district. Many of Woody's teachers were selected for district and statewide honors. Woody's schools consistently earned the highest SAT scores in the county. As if that weren't enough, Woody's schools were repeatedly honored for their commitment to sportsmanship.

As I stood at the funeral podium five months after my phone visit with his sister, I was impressed with the stories people told about him. The specifics varied with each story, but the theme was the same. Woody was a man fiercely committed to excellence. One after another, people would describe how Woody had influenced them to commit to higher standards of excellence, for their lives and their careers. Teachers told of Woody's encouragement in influencing them to pursue further education. At his urging, others had written articles and books. Over and over I heard one comment: "I wouldn't have done this if George hadn't prodded me to do it." One said, "I never thought I could speak in front of a large audience until George told me how skilled he thought I was."

Business executives, doctors, and educators all had similar comments: "The foundation for my achievement was laid during my years at Lakeshore High," or "No one in my family had a college degree, but Mr. Woodruff showed me the advantages of sticking it out until I got it done."

Many, like me, had maintained contact with him in the years following our graduation, drawn back by his message of encouragement and excellence. George believed that every person had excellence in them; all they had to do was use their unique and special talents.

Was it easy to speak at his funeral? Yes and no. It is never easy to say good-bye to a friend and mentor who has stuck by your side for three decades. Yet my task was indeed easy because I spoke with the confidence that he had been a man of influence who used his position to encourage excellence in the lives of others. He taught it and he lived it.

People like George Woodruff—people committed to building significance in others—know that half-hearted pursuits can never help a person maintain a sense of value. "Anyone can figure out how to get along," George would say, "but it takes a special person to put everything he's got toward being the best." People like George are aware that they have God-given capabilities and that they owe it to themselves (as well as those whose lives they touch) to give their all.

Although significance builders like George Woodruff never fret about what might be said at their funeral, their commitment to excellence is the message prepared long before that final time of farewell. People like George leave this world truly a better place than when they entered.

## Significance Builders

Significance builders are special people. Others love to work for and with them. And managers adore them.

People who practice these ten values are performers. They make significant contributions, whether they are Nancy the waitress or Bill the senior executive. For significance builders, title is not an issue; people are the issue.

Some companies have discovered that practicing the ten values can have an astounding impact on their organization. People love to work at a place where they are appreciated, where people tell them they are valuable, where their contribution is important. High performance companies—those that get to the top and stay there—are generally those that foster the ten values.

High performance people and high performance organizations have a lot in common. By practicing the significance principle, they find they are blessed (as do those who work with them).

It really isn't hard to understand. Wouldn't you like to work with someone who treated you with respect and recognized your value as a person and as a contributor? Before this book went to press we asked several friends and associates, many of whom work at major international firms, to read our work. We have been astonished by the one comment that almost everyone has made after they finished reading: "I would love to work at a company where I was treated like that."

Practicing the significance principle can change your life. You can impact the lives of others as you recognize their value and contributions, whether at home or at work. Truly great people dedicate their lives to building up those around them.

Say—*you* are a gifted and capable person. Why not help others discover that they, too, have great significance? We think that would be truly great.

# THE TEN VALUES OF SIGNIFICANCE BUILDERS

1. *They practice humility.* They enter relationshps with a realistic understanding of their own shortcomings and a realization that they too are human.

2. *They proactively focus on others.* They seek to understand the needs and perspectives of others.

3. *They practice integrity.* They understand that honesty and trustworthiness are bedrock qualities of any successful relationship.

4. *They deal positively with conflict.* They realize that moments of conflict can be turned into opportunities for improved communication when handled in a positive manner.

5. *They live the significance paradox.* They understand that true success is the result of first affirming the significance of others. They put team goals ahead of personal goals.

6. *They openly encourage others.* They understand the life-changing power of encouragement.

7. *They use ceremony to recognize others' significance.* They understand that the public recognition of others' accomplishments and qualities is one of the most important ways of affirming their significance.

8. *They commit to personal accountability.* They develop relationships with those who will help them maintain an ongoing practice of keeping pure motives and right relationship skills.

9. *They actively work to right wrongs.* They willingly accept feedback and look for ways to repair damage which might have been caused by their own actions.

10. *They are committed to excellence.* They realize that the quality of their work often serves as the starting point for others' success.

# NOTES

## Chapter 10

1. Everett M. Rogers, *The Diffusion of Innovations* (New York: The Free Press, 1983).
2. Michael L. Tushman, William H. Newman, and Elaine Romanelli, "Convergence and Upheaval: Managing the Unsteady Pace of Organizational Evolution," *California Management Review* 29, no. 1 (Fall 1986).
3. *Newsweek* article.
4. Rogers.
5. Jim Underwood, "Making the Break From Competitive Analysis to Strategic Intelligence," *The Journal of the Society of Competitive Intelligence,* (1994).

## Chapter 11

1. The Four P sales model is the property of David L. Rettig and is copyrighted by him. The model is presented here with his permission.